WHO'S FECKIN' WHO IN IRISH HISTORY

COLIN MURPHY

ILLUSTRATED BY BRENDAN O'REILLY

THE O'BRIEN PRESS
DUBLIN

First published 2014 by The O'Brien Press Ltd
12 Terenure Road East, Rathgar, Dublin 6, Ireland.
Tel: +353 1 4923333; Fax: +353 1 4922777
E-mail: books@obrien.ie
Website: www.obrien.ie

ISBN: 978-1-84717-632-5

1 3 5 7 8 6 4 2
14 16 18 19 17 15

Printed and bound by Scandbook AB, Sweden
The paper used in this book is produced using pulp from
managed forests.

CONTENTS

CORMAC MAC AIRT
(THIRD CENTURY)

~~~~~~

Like Michael Jackson, bits of Cormac are real and other bits were added on to improve his image. The real bits are that he was a High King of Ireland, and a very good one at that, and the unreal bits are the legends associated with him, stuff about magical cups and wolves raising him and other malarkey.

It all started for Cormac when his grandfather, Connaughtman Olc Acha, decided to get on (High King) Art Mac Cuinn's good side. So over a few tankards of ale he gave the king his daughter, Achtan – being High King could have its advantages. No sooner was she preggers with Cormac than she had a dream involving her head being chopped off, a tree sprouting from her neck and then another tree sprouting from the first tree, which would be washed away by the sea. This was interpreted as meaning that Cormac would be High King, that the sea would somehow kill him and that Art would die in battle. Well, what other way could you look at it? Sure enough the randy oul' king was chopped down by Lugaid Mac Con the next day, and he now became High King.

Legend takes over for a while and, in a tale strangely reminiscent of ancient Rome, Cormac is stolen by a she-wolf when he's a snapper and raised, Romulus and Remus-like, by wolves in a forest. But eventually a hunter finds him, takes the young lad back to his Mammy and he grows up to be a wise, merciful and handsome hunk, a fine catch for any Iron Age wench.

The next bit is probably part legend, part real. When he was 30, Cormac went to Tara, the seat of the High King, Lugaid, the guy who'd killed his father. Ancient texts describe his looks at this point:

'His hair was curled and golden. He stood in the full glow of beauty, without defect or blemish. You would think it was a shower of pearls that were set in his mouth; his symmetrical body was as white as snow; his eyes were like the sloe; his brows and eye-lashes were like the sheen of a blue-black lance.'

Or in modern Irish parlance, he was a bleedin' ride.

At Tara, he made a judgement in a case involving a woman's sheep, which had been confiscated by the High King because they'd 'eaten the queen's woad'. Painful as this sounds for the queen, woad was just a plant and Cormac decided that because the woad would grow back, as would the sheep's fleece, the woman should merely have lost her sheep's fleece, not the entire flock. The people applauded the wisdom of this so much that they gave Lugaid the boot.

I decree this to be woadjus

Unfortunately the throne was then seized by another head-the-ball called Fergus Dubdétach, who drove Cormac back to Connaught. So Cormac made an alliance with a fearsome brute called Tadg Mac Céin, who marched against Fergus. Tadg and his men chopped off Fergus's brother's head. Wrong head. Then they chopped off Fergus's other brother's head. Wrong head again. Finally they chopped off the right head.

As a reward, Cormac told Tadg that he could have any land that he could encircle in a day; he must have been a hell of a charioteer, because he got half of northern Ireland.

Wrong head   Wrong head   Right head

Finally Cormac was High King, and his Mammy's vision had been fulfilled. He married Eithne, who bore him 13 kids. Then, with Eithne no doubt banjaxed from all that child-bearing/rearing, he took a mistress called Ciarnait. Eithne, was pretty miffed, as you can imagine, so she forced Ciarnait to slave over a grindstone. Cormac is said to have built Ireland's first watermill to save her from this chore.

When not bedding Eithne or Ciarnait, Cormac battered the crap out of any rival kings. He clattered Connaught and Munster into submission and is said to have conquered parts of Britain, which makes a nice change. His reign reputedly lasted for over 30 years during which he turned Tara into a fabulous palace and seat of learning, according to the ancient Irish annals. Cormac also had a book compiled, the Psalter of Tara, which chronicled all of Irish history and the ancient Brehon Laws, which would remain in use until the English arrived seven centuries later and screwed everything up. Unfortunately the Psalter of Tara has been lost, but there might be one preserved in a bog somewhere and if you happen to find it, it's probably worth a few bob.

Poor Cormac was stuffing his gob with a salmon one night when he choked on a bone – fulfilling his Mammy's vision of his death by the sea somehow claiming him. Well, sort of.

Cormac was regarded as the greatest of all Irish kings. And the ancient texts say of him that he 'reigned majestically and magnificently'. Wonder what future texts will say about our most recent bunch of leaders/gougers?

NIALL OF THE NINE HOSTAGES

(DIED 405)

~

He may be part fact, part fiction, part mythology, but one thing we say for certain is that Niall was definitely all man. In his time he kicked the arses of all the other Irish kings, terrorised the bejaysus out of the Brits, battered the merde out of the French and even had a go at the Roman Empire. He also bedded half the cailíns in Ireland, and his sexual prowess is something we can prove scientifically.

Based on the written records, which come from documents composed long after he'd bitten the bog, Niall was said to be a descendant of a dude called Conn of the Hundred Battles, so it seems hacking people to bits was in his blood. He hailed from the Donegal/Derry area and lived around the late fourth century. His father was Eochaid Mugmedón, High King of Ireland, who had five sons by two wives, polygamy being the order of the day.

Wife 1, Mongfind, gave him four sons and Wife 2, Cairenn Chasdub, gave him Niall (Jaysus – Eochaid, Mugmedón, Mongfind and Chasdub. What is this? Dickens?). It seems that when Mongfind fell out of favour – and out of bed – with the king, she grew jealous of her successor, the now-pregnant Cairenn, and so the oul' bat made her do all the heavy work.

So one day poor Cairenn drops her sprog, and terrified of Mongfind, abandons the little mite. Luckily Niall is discovered by a poet called Torna, who raises him, and when he grows up, he returns to Tara and batters a few heads, freeing his mother from her toils. Naturally, Mongfind is seriously freaked out, so she nags Eochaid to name one of her sons as his successor. But the wise king devises various tests to choose who will plonk his arse on the throne. During one of these expeditions, the thirsty lads find a well guarded by an old hag with a face like a full skip. To drink at the well they must first kiss her. Only Niall will give the ugly old crone a proper seeing

TASTY WATER ONLY 1 KISS

to, after which she magically turns into Miss Universe 378, and not only gives Niall a drink, but the kingdom, and the guarantee that 26 of his descendants will also be king. This bit about an ugly oul' bag magically turning into a beautiful woman *before* a drink, suggests this is pure mythology, as making a horrible wagon appear gorgeous can usually only be achieved *after* drinking 20 pints.

Anyhow, after his Da died, Niall was proclaimed High King, and kindly gave smaller kingdoms to his big brothers – Connaught for you, Munster for you etc. But they weren't all happy with their lot and before you could disembowel a druid, they were at each other's throats. Niall prevailed, but didn't overcome the powerful Énnae Cennsalach, King of Leinster, and his son Eochaid.

Eochaid, it seems, had been refused hospitality by Niall's chief poet Laidceann. This was the height of bad manners apparently and reason enough to hack a few thousand men to pieces. After a few more bloody encounters (in which Eochaid impressively killed Laidceann by throwing a stone at him, burying it in his head), Niall exiled Eochaid to Scotland.

Niall then went off pillaging and raping, terrorising the poor Brits and taking countless slaves, among whom was reputed to be St. Patrick (P18). He then invaded France, and in one version, battled all the way to the Alps where he attacked Roman legions, causing the Emperor to send an ambassador to make peace. It is more likely that Niall's encounters with Romans in Briton were the source of this, and some gobshite mixed up the names 'Alba' (Britain) and 'Elpa' (Alps).

By now Niall had become numero uno in Ireland, Scotland, Britain and northern France. As the tradition was to hand over a hostage to the victorious king to ensure subservience, he got one each from Ulster, Leinster, Connaught, Munster and Meath, the Picts in Scotland, the Saxons, the Britons and the French. And if you haven't figured it out yet, ergo his trendy nickname.

Niall's reign inevitably came to a bloody end, and it is generally accepted that he was killed by Eochaid (remember the guy exiled to Scotland?). The most popular account had Niall presiding over an assembly of Picts, when Eochaid, who as we know had a fierce strong arm, shot an arrow across a Scottish valley and felled the great king, who was brought home and buried at Faughan Hill near Navan.

Niall's principal legacy was as founder of the powerful O'Neill dynasty, which would endure for hundreds of years. Oh, and then there's his offspring. Legend officially records him as having two wives, about 12 sons and an unknown number of daughters. Of course any young lass would gladly fall into the king's arms and bear his child, and it seems Niall's arms were so perpetually full of young slappers it's a wonder he ever had time to pull on his goatskin knickers and chop someone's head off. How do we know this? Well, a number of years ago a team of geneticists from Trinity College, Dublin, analysed the genes of gazillions of Irish folk, and of those of the diaspora, and announced that 20% of men in the north west had an ancient common male ancestor from the time of Niall's reign. They further estimated

Niall of the Nine Hostages and some of his 2-3 million descendants that there are three million men alive today with a bit of Niall in them, something those ancient cailíns would have also experienced. Startlingly, one in fifty New Yorkers of European descent are also descended from Niall. So whatever else, he certainly had steel in his sword.

KISS ME I'M A DESCENDANT OF NIALL OF THE NINE HOSTAGES

A fascinating footnote to this is the tale of Harvard Professor, Henry Gates Junior, who in Massachusetts in 2009, returned home, found himself locked out and tried to break in. A cop, Sgt. James Crowley, duly arrested Henry, who is African American, and a huge row erupted when Henry accused Crowley of racism. It got such press that President Obama stepped in and settled the matter over a beer in The White House. What the feck does this have to do with Niall of the Nine Hostages? Well, it seems that while making up, the Professor and Sgt. Crowley discovered that they both carried the gene identified by the Trinity College scientists – they were both the beneficiaries of Niall's ancient bed-hopping.

ST. PATRICK

(C. 387–461/2)

Y ou've probably heard of this guy already, and if you haven't, welcome to Earth. In case you're from Seti Alpha Six, he's Ireland's patron saint, along with St. Columba and St. Brigid. We're all familiar with the plastic green version of him, but what's the story with the real dude? Or was there ever really some head-the-ball going around saving us Paddies from eternal damnation and chasing away snakes etc? To give an appropriately Irish answer: yeah no.

There probably was a St. Patrick, although we don't know much about him, and what we do know mostly comes from his own 'Confessio', which he wrote when he was old and wrinkly and in which he isn't shy about telling us the wonderful job he'd done ridding us of nasty pagans. In his account, God spoke to him so often that it seems like he had God's personal mobile number. Unfortunately there was another holy geezer knocking about at the time called Palladius, also referred to as Patrick (from the Latin 'patricius', which means 'revered one' or something). The Pope sent

Palladius as Ireland's first official bishop. Somewhere in the fog of history, bits of Patrick got mixed up with bits of Palladius, and nobody knows whose bits are whose.

Here's the basics. St. Paddy was probably born around 387 at a place called Bannavem Tiburniae in either Cumbria, England, or Kilpatrick, Scotland, or Pembrokeshire, Wales, or even Brittany, France. His name was Maewyn Succat, and thanks be to Jaysus he changed that, because 'The St. Maewyn Succat's Day Parade' just doesn't have the same ring about it. His Da was a pretty well-off Roman (and a Christian), called Calpurnius, and his Ma was probably called Conchessa. But here's the thing – young Maewyn didn't believe in God!

When he was 16 a bunch of Irish pirates whisked him away into slavery in Antrim. Slemish Hill makes claim as the place where he spent six years minding sheep, although according to some he was offloaded somewhere around Mayo. His boss was a pagan gouger called Milchu. Luckily around this time, God set up his direct line to Paddy, and 'had mercy on my youthful ignorance', forgiving him his sins, presumably like impure thoughts about slave girls and binge-drinking mead. Being a very organised sort, God also arranged a ship to take him to freedom – if he could escape, walk 200 miles to the port and persuade the captain to give him a lift. Pity God couldn't have organised somewhere a bit closer, but then, God works in mysterious ways.

Anyway, the ship landed maybe in Britain or maybe Brittany, and Paddy and the pagan crew wandered around starving for a month, before our future saint prayed to God and a herd of unfortunate boar miraculously appeared. After they'd been hacked up and digested, the crew declared Paddy's God the real deal, and he was a hero.

Eventually he returned home and got stuck into his Da's bible so he could become a properly qualified Christian. Then he had another vision in which a man called Victoricus brought him a gansey-load of letters, all begging him to return to Ireland – 'Oh holy boy, come walk again among us'. You could say that this defined his career path.

So back to Ireland he goes, like a returning emigrant but without the irritating Aussie/American twang. This was about 431, and before you know it he's baptising babies, ordaining priests and persuading everyone to renounce depraved pagan practices, and become chaste, honest, moral Christians, like we've been ever since (ha ha). He also convinced lots of women to become 'virgins of Christ', much to their boyfriends' annoyance.

Eventually made a bishop, Patrick refused to accept gifts from kings, really pissing them off as these were just bribes. Neither would he accept payments for baptisms, ordinations or even from his virgins, who used to 'throw their ornaments on the altar', like the way women throw their knickers at Tom Jones. At one point he was accused of something by someone and put on trial, perhaps for 'finan-cial irregularities' (maybe he had a secret bank account in the Cayman Islands, like most rich Irish people). Presumably he was found innocent, as he wrote all about it in his 'Confessio'.

Paddy acquired a few legends along the way concerning shamrock and snakes. He's said to have used the shamrock to explain the mystery of the Holy Trinity – how the Father, the Son and the Holy Spirit were the one God. This is celebrated every year with the use of inflatable plastic shamrocks made in China. He also reputedly drove the snakes from Ireland – a pretty easy task as there were no snakes in post-glacial Ireland. Of course, the snake was a Druidic symbol, so the legend probably refers to ridding us of that shower of savages.

When exactly he went to his heavenly reward is a bit murky. It was possibly 457, but that might be when Palladius kicked the bucket. Alternatively it was in 461/2. But one source claims he cashed in his chips on March 17th, 492, aged 120. Maybe all that wandering Ireland's bogs kept him fit.

After he died there was almost war between the Ui Néill and Ulaid clans, who both wanted his body. You can just imagine the Ui Néills at one end pulling his arms and the Ulaids at the other yanking his legs. But legend has it that he was finally buried in Down Cathedral, and you can still visit his grave, although it may only contain the half of him that the Ui Néills got.

That's pretty much it. There isn't much more known about St. Paddy, except that he's given us all an excuse to get rat-arsed once a year. One suspects he wouldn't be deliriously happy about that legacy.

ST. BRIGID

(C. 451–523)

~

Another of Ireland's patron saints, although there's no day off to get trollied in her honour. She's also called Bridget, Bridgit or Bride meaning 'exalted one'. There was a pagan goddess, also called Brigid, who also supposedly possessed healing powers, like our Brigid, and St. Brigid's feast day, February 1st, also happens to be the date of the Imbolg, the pagan Spring festival.

Her father was a pagan guy called Dubhthach, a king in Leinster, and her mother was Brocca, a slave. In other versions, her father was also a slave kidnapped by Irish pirates from warm, sunny Lusitania (Portugal) and hauled back to wet and windy Ireland. After her birth, probably in Louth, a druid told her father to call her after the pagan goddess, and then tried to feed her. However she puked all over the nasty pagan, which was taken as a sign of his impurity (i.e. he wasn't a Christian) but which was probably a case of gastroenteritis caused by eating undercooked pig's eye or something.

As she grew up, Brigid started healing people left, right and centre. She was also a beauty and lads were soon blowing

Yep... looks like we've got ourselves a saint here.

wolf-whistles and generally making a nuisance of themselves. But Brigid had promised herself to God, so the lads were rightly miffed. And it wasn't beyond her to cast the odd curse. One poor eejit called Bacene, who made fun of her for remaining a virgin was cursed so: 'Your eyes will burst in your head'. Two exploding eyes later, Bacene got the message.

Brigid was renowned for her charity and kept giving away her parents' stuff to the poor. This reached a climax when she gave her father's jewel-encrusted sword to a leper. Dubhthach was like a mad thing and finally granted her wish, packing her off to a convent. Clever girl.

She was ordained a nun soon after and given abbatial powers, which was a big deal as she was only 17. Off she went on her travels, convincing lots of young girls to become nuns. She founded a small oratory in Kildare that eventually became a major centre for pilgrimage and learning, two monastic institutions, one for the boys, one for the girls, and also an art school, which produced a Book of Kells-type masterpiece, called the Book of Kildare, which was lost, but which was said to be 'a work of angelic skill'.

Biddy was a busy nun. Her monasteries and schools became famed throughout Europe and soon there were all sorts of head-the-balls turning up with

funny accents. She actually became best buddies with Mr Big of the Irish monastic world, St. Paddy (P18) – it was said of 'there was so great a friendship of charity that they had but one heart and mind.'

Among Brigid's top miracle hits were curing a leper with a mug of blessed water, and curing two deaf sisters by rubbing some of their blood mixed with water on their necks. She could also multiply foods and control the weather. Handy tricks to have up your abbess's sleeve.

Her most famous miracle is the one with the cloak. She wanted a local king to donate land for a convent, but the mean oul' shite refused. So after a word with God, she tried again, asking the king for 'as much land as my cloak will cover.' Of course the sucker agreed. So four co-nuns grabbed a corner of the cloak each and started walking in different directions,

26

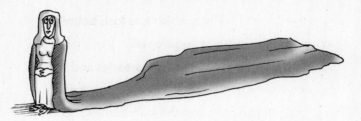

and the cloak magically stretched out to cover the size of a football pitch. The king converted and the convent was built.

Then there's the St. Brigid's Cross. You know the one with the square middle bit and four arms radiating out? A pagan chieftain was dying and Brigid arrived to convert him before he ended up in hell. But he wasn't having any of it and was ranting and raving. So she started absent-mindedly weaving the rushes on the floor together and made a cross, and miraculously, the chieftain became transfixed by this and converted in the nick of time, saving himself from eternal roasting.

As a thank you for all the good PR, God spared her till she was 72, an impressive age at the time. She was originally buried, it is said, alongside St. Patrick and St. Columba in Downpatrick Cathedral, in Down, but a few centuries later some knights removed her skull (yeuch) and gave it as a gift to King Denis of Portugal.

Perhaps he'd have preferred a nice jumper or a box of chocolates, but there you go.

The skull is today in a fancy metal box in the Church of John the Baptist in Lisbon.

Brigid also has a gazillion places around Ireland named after her – there are 19 Kilbrides alone ('Kil' meaning 'church'), as well as places like Brideswell, Rathbride, Templebreedy. And she's an international hit too, having had artworks, churches etc. named in her honour in Scotland, France, England, Belgium, Germany, Italy, Holland, Portugal, Spain and the USA.

And all this despite never having been officially canonised. You see, she became a saint because so many people revered her that the Vatican thought 'Oh what the hell,' and officially recognised her. The slave girl from Louth did well for herself.

ST. BRENDAN THE NAVIGATOR/THE VOYAGER

(C. 484–C. 577)

～～～

Did an Irishman discover the Americas a millennium before Columbus? Who knows? There's a possibility that St. Brendan did. Of course, this 'discovering America' bullshit ignores the fact that there were already indigenous people living there for yonks. But we digress.

St. Brendan was a real guy, a Kerryman, born around 484, to the joy of parents Finnlug and Cara. Originally they'd planned to name him 'Mobhí', but changed their minds due to portents in the sky or some malarkey, so called him 'Broen Finn', meaning 'Fair Drop', as in 'Jaysus, I've had a fair drop and I'm rat arsed'. No, only kidding. It probably meant he was fair-haired. He was baptised by a holy oul' lad called St. Erc, educated by a holy oul' wan called St.

Ita and then by another holy guy called St. Jarlath, so it was perhaps inevitable he'd end up a holy Joe himself. Incidentally, St. Ita was said to embody the 'six virtues of womanhood' – wisdom, purity, musical ability, gentle speech and needle skills. Well, at least Irish girls still have the wisdom.

Besides the call of God, he also heard the call of the sea, and before you could say a Hail Mary, he was off sailing around Ireland, converting pagans and

founding monasteries all over the gaff. Not content with saving the souls of Paddy pagans, he also journeyed to Wales, Scotland and Brittany. Clearly the travel bug had bitten.

At some point in his thirties or forties, Brendan decided to sail into the vast sea to the west. This is where fact and fiction become somewhat inter-twined, or to put it another way, banjaxed. Most of the legend of Brendan's voyage was written centuries after he died, and it has to be taken with a container ship of sea salt. There are elements of Irish mythology in it, not to mention Greek mythology and various other mythologies.

Brendan set off from the foot of Mount Brandon (hence its name) with a number of followers, either 12, 14, 60 or 150, depending on who you believe. His boat was made of wattle (bits of sticks tied together) covered in hides. On their adventure they encounter a land where 'demons throw down lumps of fiery slag from an island with rivers of gold fire [and] great crystal pillars'. Some say this is a description of Iceland. Fair enough. They also find an island where food has been left out for them, but mys-teriously, there are no people only an Ethiopian Devil, whatever the hell that is. But now it gets a

GREETINGS FROM PARADISE OF BIRDS ISLAND

bit freaky, because next up is the Paradise of Birds inhabited by birds, who, wait for it, recite psalms to the Lord. Talking birds? Ok, let's move on.

Along comes the island of Ailbe, inhabited by ageless silent monks. After spending Christmas here and having a bit of turkey and pud, the voyagers depart. They have various other adventures with sea

The Isle of Blacksmiths

creatures, birds bringing prophesies and an island of blacksmiths (yes, that's right, blacksmiths, for the love of Jaysus). On one small island, they light a fire only to discover the 'island' is actually a whale. You'd think the eejits would notice that the ground was a bit smooth and rubbery, but no. Then along comes a 'gryphon', like the 'griffin' of Greek mythology – half lion and half eagle. Anyway, it's about to devour them when another fabulous bird bates the shite out of it. Next, they find Judas sitting on a rock in the middle of nowhere. It seems he gets a day off from Hell on Sunday and gets to spend it here – we all need a break every now and then.

The Gryphon

Among the most fabulous places they discover was one they called St. Brendan's Island – a beautiful place covered with luxuriant vegetation. In the centuries before Columbus, the legend of Brendan's Voyage had become so widespread across Europe that this mysterious island was actually marked on maps and there were reported sightings of it up to the 19th century. It may have been the Faroes, Canaries, Madeira, the Azores or it could all be a big pile of baloney. On the other hand, as some maintain, it could also have been America. The absence in America of an ancient sign reading 'St. Brendan was here. You'll never beat the Irish!' makes this theory tricky to prove. Still, if you ignore the sea creatures, blacksmiths, immortal monks, gryphons, etc., it may just be possible that old Brenno beat Columbus to the line by 1000 years. In the 1970s, an English chap by the name of Tim Severin built a reconstruction of Brendan's boat, and managed to reach America in it to show the voyage was possible. Fair play to you, Tim.

Back from his fab voyage, normal service was resumed and Brendan founded loads more monasteries, most famously at Clonfert in Galway and Ardfert in Kerry. Brendan's final voyage was a visit to his sis, Briga, in Galway, where he died. Apparently, fearing that the peasantry would try to nab bits of him as keepsakes, he'd asked to be quickly laid to rest in Clonfert, before his leg, ear or some other unspeakable part of him ended up on someone's mantelpiece. So his corpse was secretly whisked away and buried beside the church. There's a headstone at Clonfert Cathedral claiming to be his grave. Yeah, right.

There's no doubt Brendan existed, that he sailed a lot and that he established lots of monasteries and so on, and he is officially recognised as a saint by the Catholic, Anglican and Eastern Orthodox Church. And he may even have discovered America. If he did, he deserves a big slap on the back. It would be fitting, wouldn't it, considering we've sent about a billion other people there since.

There's a whole heap of stuff named after or written about Brendan. Mountains, churches, songs, poems, films, documentaries, books, you name it. There's even a rock song by a Canadian band, The Lowest of the Low, called 'St. Brendan's Way'. It appears on an album called *Shakespeare My Butt*. Brendan's also the patron saint of sailors, and of scuba divers. Perhaps he should also be the patron saint of emigrants?

IVAR THE BONELESS
(DIED C. 873)

Strictly speaking, the intriguingly named Viking may not even have been born here, but his name is worth a laugh, so let's make him an honorary Paddy.

Ivar ruled over the Uí Ímair Viking dynasty, which existed from the mid-ninth to the late tenth century, which meant he had lots of Britons under his thumb, so he can't have been all bad. His kingdom was one of the most powerful in the Viking world, stretching from the Hebrides, through Scotland, across Northern England, Wales, the Isle of Man and Ireland. It was said of Ivar that he was 'fair, strong, wise and a great warrior', and as he made his conquests the local gentry would gift him their daughters to appease him, one of whom was called Aud the Deepminded. The Boneless and the Deepminded? So what was their unlucky firstborn known as – 'the Boneminded'?

$$\left(\frac{\left(\pi x - 3^2\right)^2}{(t+D)^2}\right)$$

Aud the Deepminded

Besides his gold-plundering, virgin-stealing, all-conquering adventures, the most intriguing thing about Ivar has to be his name, which has been a matter of some speculation. One of the most curious suggestions is that, in the baby-making department, poor Ivar was about as erect as a length of overcooked linguini. This is unlikely, however, as he had several wives and was frequently required to ravish a wench or two to prove his leadership skills. Another theory is that Ivar was incredibly flexible in battle, and could slice the kidneys out of one

It could be worse... He could have erectile disfunction

opponent while at the same time castrating a second guy behind him. A further theory is that his name was screwed up in translation and it actually means 'Ivan the Legless.' This is much more plausible, as anyone who's ever spent any time in Dublin any weekend can confirm. Taken literally, though, it may imply that poor Ivar had no legs, and there's evidence that he was borne on his shield by his warriors. But then Vikings usually carried their glorious warriors about on their shields, so unless we assume that every Viking king had no legs, it is unlikely this explains the nick-name. And it is a bit hard to imagine Ivar being 'a great warrior' and charging into battle on a couple of stumps, which sounds like a Monty Python sketch.

Ivar met a nasty end in 873 when he 'died of a sudden hideous disease... thus it pleased God.' After which he was undoubtedly known as Ivar the Lifeless.

BRIAN BORU

(C. 941–1014)

In school we all learned that Brian Boru was the Irish hero that saved us from the nasty horrible Vikings and not only that, he was so pious that he was at prayer when a Viking buried a hatchet in his head. So not only did he enjoy Irish hero status but almost saint-hood as well. But that's mostly a load of oul' bollox. Having said that, there were elements of truth in what was battered into us. Brian did put an end to any serious remnants of Viking power and, to be fair to the fecker, he was arguably one of Ireland's greatest military leaders, so he does deserve some of the legendary status.

Many people also mistakenly believe that Brian was a Jackeen, primarily because his most famous battle was in Clontarf. Others think he was from the Meath area because he was a High King. But no, Brian was a big Culchie galoot. Think of him like a big hairy Fianna Fáil cute hoor, but with a helmet and a shield.

Brian hailed from Killaloe in beautiful Clare, the Da being Cennétig Mac Lorcáin, the local king, and the Mammy being Bé Binn inion Urchadh (possibly 'Binny' for short, as saying things like 'Is me shirt washed yet, Bé Dinn inion Urchadh?' could be a bit of a mouthful). Poor Binny was hacked to death during a Norse raid when Brian was a youngfella, which for some reason gave him a dislike of the dirty big Scandinavians.

His big brother, Mathgamain (whose name evolved into 'McMahon'), inherited the kingship. Their main foe was a Viking mentaller called Ivar of Limerick. When Mathgamain agreed a truce with Ivar, Brian would have none of it and took to the hills, launching guerrilla-style attacks against Norse settlements. He was a fierce tactician and often defeated vastly superior numbers, leaving Ivar with a right puss. Brian's fame spread and Mathgamain decided it was time to kiss and make up with his brother, and so told Ivar to feck off. The brothers then marched on Ivar's forces,

So, the plan is for a battalion of skull-crushers to go here, and a division of disembowellers will go here.

beat the crap out of them and sent Ivar legging it out of Ireland. But a few years later he snuck back and killed Mathgamain. Brian then challenged Ivar to open combat, during which he dispatched the Norseman to Valhalla.

Now king, he decided to take on his brother's old enemies and expand his kingdom a tad. At the time there were over 100 local kings in Ireland. Some were quite powerful, but others' kingdoms were roughly the size of a soggy beermat. Brian led his armies to victory after victory, and in 978, he defeated the King of Cashel and became King of Munster.

But he wasn't finished yet and his gaze turned towards Leinster, Meath and Connaught, where there were lots more little and large Irish kings and smelly

Norsemen. Brian cleverly used the Shannon as a means of getting his armies up around Connaught and Meath, and it was through this he developed his tactical skills, by combining naval and land forces to encircle his enemies. His raids went on for 15 years from 982, which really pissed off the High King, Máel Sechnaill mac Domnaill.

Now poor Máel has really been robbed of his rightful place in history, because in 980, at the Battle of Tara, he inflicted a crushing defeat on Olaf Cuaran, Viking King of Dublin. Olaf was the last powerful Norse king in Ireland and it was this victory and not Brian's at Clontarf that ended any serious Viking power. But unfortunately Máel's name is a bit tricky to pronounce whereas Brian Boru has a bit of alliteration going for it and easily trips off the tongue, and such are the whims of history.

In 997, Máel Sechnaill agreed a truce, Brian getting basically the bottom half of Ireland and Máel getting the rest. This didn't go down well with Máel's former allies and so they gave him the boot as King of Leinster (although he was still High King of Ireland) and replaced him with another Máel – Máel Morda Mac Murchada, who launched a rebellion against Brian and his lads. Máel Morda allied himself with his Viking cousin, Sigtrygg Silkbeard, who was the incumbent Viking King of Dublin, and in 999, the opposing armies met at the Battle of Glenmáma in Wicklow.

According to ancient texts, the rebels had the shite kicked out of them by Brian, losing 7000 men. But Brian decided to be merciful to the Viking leader and not only allowed him remain as King of Dublin, but gave him one of his daughters in marriage. He probably thought it was a good way to stop her free-loading off him. He also took the young Sigtrygg's Mammy, called Gormflaith, as his own bride, and at the time it must have been one big happy family because Gormflaith was also Máel Morda's sister. Got all that?

Now, getting back to the other Máel, the High King, with whom Brian had made a truce years before-hand. Well, Brian decided he wasn't happy with only half of Ireland, he now wanted the bleedin' lot. So the fecker conveniently forgot about the truce and launched an attack on Meath. In 1002, it is recorded that Máel Sechnaill threw up his hands and said he'd had enough of this High King shite. And so Brian was finally acknowledged by most of Ireland as High King.

The only bit left was Ulster, and those northern boys weren't going to quit without a fight.

It took 10 long years before Brian overcame the gansey-load of Ulster kingdoms. He did it by again combining land and sea forces, attacking along the coast while his land forces trapped the enemy from the other side. He consolidated his power by getting the Catholic Church onside, first of all, by giving them loads of free gold. He made Armagh the religious capital and forced others to make regular contributions, so the church decided it would be handy to keep Brian in power, as he made them lots of dosh. He also rebuilt churches that the Vikings had banjaxed and generally made himself best buddies with all the bishops.

But there was trouble brewing. Despite the fact that Brian was married to Gormflaith, his brother-in-law Máel Morda, still King of Leinster, was not a happy camper. His defeat by Brian in 999 was still nagging away, and in 1012, he decided it was time for a return match. After attacking Meath he returned to Dublin knowing the Brian would soon come, hungry for payback. He ordered Sigtrygg to leg it to Orkney and the Isle of Man to recruit a huge shower of savages. It should be noted that Sigtrygg and his Norse pals had long since assimilated into Irish society and were only really Viking in name, so the Vikings who Sigtrygg was trying to recruit to defend Dublin were a bunch of mercenaries, who were basically in it for the loot and not to defend any Irish Viking kingdom. So when Brian faced the combined forces in Dublin, it wasn't to free Ireland from Viking oppression, but to take on another Irish king, a collection of Irish-born guys of Viking extraction, and a bunch of hired thugs bent on a bit of pillaging and raping. The fact was that Brian and Máel's confrontation might have been known as the First Irish Civil War, with a load of Viking yobs thrown in. Oh, and one other thing: Brian actually had a bunch of his own Vikings fighting for him as well.

Let's not go into the detail of the Battle of Clontarf too much. You know how these

Er, Brian. Any suggestion for all these severed limbs?

44

things went generally – Olaf chops off Paddy's hand, Paddy chops off Olaf's arm, Olaf chops off Paddy's leg, Paddy chops off Olaf's head. Multiply this by about 10,000 and you've got the general picture of limbs and heads absolutely littering the promenade at Clontarf. The whole bleedin' mess (literally) took place on April 23rd 1014, which was Good Friday, giving it a religious significance and meaning that God was definitely on Brian's side. We do seem to like staging our big battles around Easter.

Here's a couple of interesting bits about the battle. It lasted just a day, but began at dawn with the opposing forces just slagging each other, the Irish yelling things like 'Hey, Olaf, I hear your wife would

D'you think I should mention that it's the Easter Bank Holiday?

get up on a stiff breeze!' to which a Viking would reply 'Hey Mick, your mother's a walking argument for contraception.' And so on. Then, every now and again, the two slaggers would march out and hack away at each other until someone was dead, while their buddies cheered them on, much like a hurling match. Soon after breakfast, they got to killing each other en masse and, as we all know, Brian's army knocked the crap out of the Vikings who lost 6000 men to Brian's 4000.

Another episode was that involving Ulf the Quarrelsome, Brian's brother. During the battle, Ulf encountered Brodir, the leader of the Isle of Man Vikings and the pair of them battered away at each other but without a decisive victor. After the battle, an ancient text records that Brodir sneaked into Brian's tent while he was praying and murdered him. But for all we know Brian died as a result of a heart attack after a celebratory shag with Gormflaith – he was in his seventies, after all. Whatever the truth, Brodir was officially blamed and an ancient Viking text recounts that Ulf, now feeling particularly quarrelsome, tracked down Brodir and decided to inflict a nasty death in revenge (and if you're eating a sambo you might want to stop before you read on): 'Ulf the Quarrelsome cut open Brodir's belly, and led him round and round a tree, and wound all his entrails out of him, and he did not die before they were all drawn out.' Lovely.

After Brian's death, Máel Sechnaill mac Domnaill became High King again. And Brian Boru became a legend. One of the reasons for this was because, in the centuries of English oppression, Brian was portrayed as the hero who freed Ireland from tyranny, and if we got rid of one bunch of dirty gougers, we could get rid of another. Unfortunately it would be yonks before we got another military strategist to match the crafty Clareman.

DERMOT MACMURROUGH
(C. 1110–1 MAY 1171)

~~~

If Dermot MacMurrough came back and saw his name in this Anglicised form (instead of Diarmait Mac Murchada), well, the oul' fecker would only have himself to blame, because Dermot's the eejit who invited the Brits to Ireland in the first place, and like a nasty rash in a private area, they simply wouldn't go away. In fact they hung around causing misery, death and destruction for over seven centuries. As a result, the history books have pretty much painted Dermo as a traitor to Ireland, but to be honest, the poor eejit got a bit of a raw deal.

He was born around 1110, son of the King of Leinster, but his Da was dispatched by a Viking hatchet when he was 14 and his elder brother then became king. Around this time the only things on Dermot's mind were probably teenage pimples and trying to grab a grope with some young wenches. But his brother went and popped his clogs after only a year, leaving Dermot as King of Leinster, aged just 15. This might have seemed grand to him as he could now command any wench to his chamber and he could drink mead all day. But almost before he'd time to burst one of his royal spots, he was ousted, because the High King of Ireland feared that Dermot would become a rival and sent one of his allies, a nasty piece of work named Tigernán Ua Ruairc, to depose him. This sparked an enmity between Dermot, the High

King and Ua Ruairc that would last decades and ultimately lead to the English arriving.

If you find any underpants in there, they're mine.

It took six years for Dermot to get his throne back and, by now, he was bucking mad. He'd become pretty ruthless on his way back to power. Among the most notorious of his acts was to abduct and 'despoil' the abbess of Kildare so he could appoint one more sympathetic to his cause. As the ancient texts record: 'The nun herself was taken and put into a man's bed.'

In the years after, he strengthened his hold on power, kicking the shite out of several armies and, if he captured an enemy, one of his favourite punishments was to blind them. You did not want to get on the wrong side of this head-the-ball, who, it was said 'preferred to be feared by all rather than loved'. No kidding.

Then in 1152, Dermot decided to attack the kingdom of Breifne (roughly Cavan and Leitrim), which was ruled by Tigernán Ua Ruairc – yep, the same one who had ousted him years before. He decided that it would really piss Tigernán off to kidnap his wife, Derbforgaill, and if you believe the Annals of Clonmacnoise, he did this because 'he wished to satisfy his insatiable, carnal and adulterous lust'. The chances are though that Derbforgaill didn't offer too much resistance to Dermot, as it's recorded that during her 'abduction' she had time to pack her dresses, lingerie and jewellery, and also to pile all her furniture on carts, and she would live contentedly with Dermot for yonks. Turns out, her family had always wanted an alliance with Dermot, anyway. Still, the hubby was not pleased, and Tigernán began plotting revenge, although he was evidently a slow plotter as it took 14 years.

In 1166, Tigernán Ua Ruairc and his buddy, the High King himself, Ruaidrí Ua Conchobair, marched against Dermot on the pretext of avenging the kidnap of Tigernán's missus. Little did he know it, but the High King's action meant that he would earn himself the unwanted title of 'The Last High King of Ireland'. Dermot was deposed and legged it to England, where he politely asked King Henry II to lend him troops so he could go back and batter the bejaysus out of his enemies. If only he'd known what he was starting!

So Dermot was allowed to recruit a gang of Norman yahoos who landed in Ireland on May 1st 1169 and succeeded in getting back some of Dermot's power and lands. But he was a greedy fecker and he made an alliance with another Norman, Richard de Clare, nicknamed Strongbow, by granting him the hand of his daughter, Aoife, not to mention all her other bits. Like with most weddings, strife and misery were to follow and, sure enough, Strongbow arrived with more gougers in 1170 and they quickly battered

Aoife meets Strongbow

their way from Wexford to Dublin. The following year, King Henry himself landed with a much larger army at Waterford and, before you know it, half the country was overrun by burly guys with funny accents, shouting things like: 'Ere, that wench is a nice bi' o' stuff, wot?'

The English arrive in Ireland.

Dermot died in 1171, leaving lots of nice land and wealth to his descendants, and leaving seven centuries of misery and mayhem to the rest of us. Thanks a bunch.

RUAIDHRÍ UA CONCHOBHAIR (RORY O'CONNOR)

(1116–1198)

Considering the dodgy times he lived in, it's hard to believe that Rory lived to be 82. From his teen years Rory aspired to the big seat – High King of Ireland – so the young galoot was nothing if not ambitious. And while he did make it to the top, his place in Irish history was not secured by particularly heroic deeds, but because the word 'Last' would also be glued on to his title.

Rory and family hailed from Connaught. His Da, Turlough, was King of Connaught and would eventually become the 'Third Last High King of Ireland'. He was a randy oul' git, was Turlough, and fathered at least 20 sons and Jaysus-knows how many young-wans, so Rory was well down the pecking order in terms of inheriting the throne. And it was not one big happy family, which is hardly surprising as there must have been terrible rows in the mornings, all trying to get into the jacks at the same time. Rory wasn't exactly his Da's pet either – two of his other brothers got to be 'Tánaiste' (which was what the heir to the

Hey! See the big Tánaiste!

Would you look at that Tánaiste eejit!

TOP QUALITY SALIVA FOR SALE.

throne was called, whereas nowadays it's a pretty useless government position that Michael O'Leary described as being 'not worth a bucket of spit'). But through various battles, treachery, kidnapping, butchery and so on, Rory got his pesky brothers out of the way, so that when Turlough kicked the bucket in 1156, Rory grabbed the throne.

Considering that he had at least 13 children, it seems he also grabbed a thing or two else. But he still had his eye on the big one, and in 1159 he made his first attempt to unseat Muircheartach Mac Lochlainn (the Second Last High King of Ireland). But he made a bollox of it and another seven years would pass before Mac Lochlainn had his own guts spilled by someone else, making way for Rory to plant his 40-year-old arse on the throne.

If he thought that it would be all medieval banquets and busty wenches pouring mead from then on, he was disappointed. There were still lots of annoying kings around the gaff who didn't particularly like him, in particular Dermot MacMurrough (P47), King of Leinster. So naturally Rory attacked

Dermot and sent him packing. Dermot was soon back with a bunch of Normans from England, beating the crap out of Rory's armies. But getting a favour from the English King Henry II was like getting one from Don Corleone: he'd expect something in return, and it turned out the royal geebag expected nothing less than Ireland itself.

Most other Irish kings succumbed almost without a squawk, but Rory staged a number of attacks on Strongbow and his Norman pals, and for a while he had them shitting planks. But the crafty feckers launched a surprise counter-attack – so surprising, in fact, that poor Rory was taking his annual bath at the time and had to leg it in the nip. He retreated to

Ruaidhrí! There's some English people here to see you!

55

Connaught, presumably finding some clothes along the way, and there he festered while pondering his next move.

Meantime Strongbow et al were getting to like their new home and soon established a nice big colony. Dermot was pushing up daisies by 1171 and King Henry II now got worried that Strongbow was getting a bit too comfy. He decided to come to Ireland himself in case his compatriot started getting ideas above his station. The remaining Irish kings submitted to Henry, but it would be four years before Rory had gotten over his huff enough to agree to the Treaty of Windsor with King Henry.

The treaty gave Rory a kingdom consisting of everywhere outside Leinster, Meath, Dublin and Waterford and all he had to do was pay Henry 'one cow hide for each of his 10 cattle', which sounds like a pretty decent bargain. Unfortunately Rory misinterpreted the treaty, believing he was still High King, whereas Henry saw him as a two-bit Paddy king who he could squash any time. And the Normans in Ireland ignored the treaty anyway and began snatching bits of Rory's land as well as tossing up square, boring-looking castles all over the place, many of which are still standing. And over the next decades the Normans started marrying Irish cailíns and adopting Irish customs and even the language, so that after a while, it was hard to tell the incomers from the Micks.

Meantime, while the Normans were busy siring little Irish-Normans, poor Rory's influence, power and territory was shrivelling, like the man himself. By the age of 70 he'd had his fill of royal power and sought solace in Cong Monastery where the old bowsie lingered on for another 12 years. He finally handed in his regal cards in 1198, ending the succession of Irish High Kings that had endured all the way back into the mists of mythology. There were a couple of would-be High Kings in the following centuries,

Father... I comitted treachery... I butchered... I gouged out a few eyes...

but the reality was that Ireland was, for the first time in history, under the thumb of a bunch of foreigners.

ST. LAURENCE O'TOOLE

(C. 1128–1180)

One of Ireland's most revered saints – after St. Patrick and Ray Houghton, that is. Not only a miracle worker, Larry was also fairly handy at keeping warring kings from cutting each other's throats, and he reformed the Irish Church and gave a large bunch of clerical bowsies the boot. We could have used him in recent times.

God, I promise I'll be a saint if you get me out of here.

He was born into a posh family in Castledermot, Kildare, his father Muirchertach was a kind of mini-king to Dermot

MacMurrough (P47), King of Leinster. When just 10, poor Larry was sent as a hostage to MacMurrough to ensure loyalty. Unfortunately Muirchertach went and upset the boss somehow and the poor little fecker was thrown into a dungeon for two years. It was during this time of misery that he discovered God, and who wouldn't?

After his father and Dermot had buried the hatchet, a very thin, pale Larry was sent to Glendalough where he decided to stay, and before you could say an Our Father, he was appointed Abbot, aged just 24. He was reputedly a pretty decent and good-looking dude, tall and graceful, charismatic and charitable. He became an Augustinian monk, and so gave up anything remotely resembling pleasure, much like most of Ireland after recent budgets. But he was already the abstemious type anyway – he often went for days on bread and water. As a means of atonement, he wore a hair shirt next to his skin, a wojus scratchy yoke made of coarse animal hair. Whatever rocks your boat. In later life, he would throw lavish banquets, but used to add red colour to his own cup of water to make it look like wine, so he wouldn't spoil the party mood (it's said that many Irish restaurants do something similar).

But Larry hadn't finished scaling the ecclesiastical ladder and by age 34 he was Archbishop of Dublin – surprisingly with the support of both Dermot MacMurrough (who had married Larry's sister) and Ruaidhrí Ua Conchobhair (P52), future High King, who hated each other's guts. The first Irishman to get the job (they'd all been Scandinavians 'till then), he quickly began to reform the Irish church. A letter from the era shows how arseways the church had become:

'...things have been reported that displease us: namely that every man abandons his wife at his will and takes to himself another wife who may be of his own kin or the kindred of the abandoned wife so that the law of marriage has become a law of fornication; infants are baptised without chrism (holy oil); holy orders are given by bishops for money...'

So basically all our men were randy, unfaithful yahoos, our babies were sinners and our bishops a bunch of medieval cute hoors. Anyway, Larry set us straight with the Pope's blessing, found time to feed

Dublin's teeming poor, house the city's abandoned orphans and even lay the foundation stone for Christ Church Cathedral. He was one popular head-the-ball.

Along came the Norman invasion, thanks to his brother-in-law, Dermot. It's safe to say things were a bit frosty at family get-togethers after that. As the Normans approached, the people of Dublin feared they'd all be mincemeat by morning, so they begged the bishop to go and make peace. While he was conducting negotiations, the treacherous Normans sneaked around behind his back, breached the walls and began hacking poor Dubs to bits. Hearing the screams he quickly legged it back and tried to per-suade the Norman brutes to stop chopping, burning and raping, pointing out that, if they carried on, when Dublin was theirs, they'd have no houses to live in, no subjects to command and no girls left to have a bit of craic with. The dumb invaders scratched their heads and desisted. And thus he became famed as 'Larry the Peace Maker'.

His new-found skill was soon in demand all over the place. He was the choice of Henry II to conduct the negotiations for the Treaty of Windsor (see P56) and even succeeded in getting the High King some of his power back for the price of a few cow hides. Larry would have been handy dealing with the EU about the national debt.

Laurence, it's Merkel on line one.

At one point during the negotiations, he travelled to Canterbury and the shrine of St. Thomas Becket (the guy King Henry was reputed to have had bumped off). In the middle of the Mass, some religious looper decided to give the church another martyr alongside Becket, and ran up and bashed Larry over the head with a club. The story goes that the bishop appeared dead, but got up and asked for water, which he blessed and then used to wash his bleeding noggin. Miraculously, the bleeding stopped instantly – Lawrence could even perform miracles on himself! Either that or he'd just gotten a scratch. Anyway, he pardoned the looper, and finished the Mass. He was an instant hit and his fame spread far and wide as a merciful, forgiving miracle-worker.

In 1179 Larry went to Rome and was made Papal Legate. When he came back he continued to kick clerical arses, and removed hundreds of dodgy bishops and priests from their posts. The following year he left our shores again, first to go to England and then to Normandy, intending to give King Henry a good slapping for breaches of the Treaty of Windsor. Unfortunately he never made it, as he fell ill and died on November 14th, 1180. His last words were to his fellow Irish: 'Alas, you poor, foolish people, what will you do now? Who will take care of you in your trouble?' Good question.

He was buried in Normandy, although his heart was removed first for dispatch to Christ Church in Dublin. He was barely cold in the ground when the miracles attributed to him started to pile up. Prayers to him cured among other things the black plague, irritable bowel syndrome, Creutzfeldt-Jakob's disease and erectile dysfunction, to name but a few. There were so many miracles that the Pope canonised him after just 45 years, something of a record. St. Larry's heart remained in a shrine in Dublin for over 800 years until March 3rd, 2012, when some geebag stole it, for God knows what reason. Maybe he/she prays to it for a miracle to cure him/her from eternal stupidity.

Nowadays Larry's name is venerated by a gansey-load of schools, athletics clubs, pipe bands and so on. Oh, and a handy bit of knowledge for the pub quizzes: he's also the patron saint of Dublin.

GERALD MÓR FITZGERALD, 8TH EARL OF KILDARE

(1456–1513)

~~~

A real bigwig, Gerald's nicknames (Garret the Great, Gearóid Mór, The Great Earl, The Uncrowned King of Ireland) give a clue to his standing. However, he wasn't standing for total Irish freedom, but a kind of version of it, where the English would leave us alone if we didn't act the maggot too much.

He was a descendant of the Normans who'd conquered Ireland a few centuries earlier. These

Anglo-Normans took a liking to our ways (who could blame them?), and ended up speaking the language and marrying the cailíns. After a few generations they were 'more Irish than the Irish themselves'. While some of them remained loyal to the English Crown – including the FitzGeralds of Kildare – others wanted their own little dynasties, so there was a lot of inter-clan slagging, disembowelling, and general ructions.

At 21, Gerald's Da died and he became Lord Deputy of Ireland, i.e. the Crown's head honcho. He also inherited the title Earl of Kildare. But the following year King Edward IV decided that Gerald was too powerful and that an Englishman would be better suited to the job of Lord Deputy. The feckin' cheek. The Irish lords were outraged and refused to deal with Gerald's replacement, some twit called Lord Grey of Codnor, and the king had to reverse his decision. Gerald kept the job after Henry VII became king in 1485, and such was his power that Henry was a bit nervy about kicking him out.

Supposedly a man of exceptional charisma, Gerald was 'of tall stature and goodly presence; very liberal and merciful; mild in his government; passionate, but easily appeased'. During his reign, which was one of Ireland's few brief eras of virtual independence, he built castles and rebuilt towns that had been banjaxed during previous wars.

Then in 1487 he really pissed off Henry VII when he decided to support a pretender to the throne called Lambert Simnel, who was all of 10. Simnel had no real claim to the Crown, but was a double of another kid who did, and various power-hungry English guys were using the poor little gobshite as a puppet. So they brought him to Ireland for the 'coronation of Edward VI' in Christ Church Cathedral. Afterwards, various lords plotted an invasion of England with the poor Simnel at their head, probably pooping his short pants. Unfortunately they had the crap knocked out of them at the Battle of Stoke Field. Lots of leaders lost heads, but King Henry was merciful to Simnel, and gave him a job as kitchen spit-turner in his palace. He was also merciful to Gerald and let him have his old job back, as basically Henry needed him on his side. Later Henry would comment that the Irish would crown an ape to secure power. And maybe he was right. Just look at some of our past Taoisigh.

Eventually in 1494, Gerald's Irish enemies ganged up on him, seized power and sent him over to the Tower of London in chains as a traitor. But Gerald wasn't called 'The Great' for nothing. At his trial he convinced King Henry that his enemies in Ireland were the real bad guys, and bob's your uncle, Henry re-appointed him as Lord Deputy and sent him back to Ireland to kick arse. As a bonus, Henry also gave him his cousin, Elizabeth St. John, as a replacement wife, as his original one had died while he was banged up.

Back in Ireland, Gerald set about wielding his power with renewed energy, suppressing a rebellion in Cork in 1499 that was inspired by another pretender to the throne, a guy called Perkin Warbeck. But Gerald wasn't going to make the same mistake twice; he crushed Warbeck's supporters and hanged Cork's mayor.

Five years later the Burke clan of Connaught declared war. Gerald duly crushed them to a pulp, as well as the O'Neill clan in Belfast and the Bisset clan in Antrim. But his crushing days were almost over; in 1513, while suppressing yet another rebellion by the O'Carroll clan in Kildare, he was struck by an arrow, and Garret the Great suddenly became Garret the Dead.

Legend says that Gerald and his army slumber beneath the Curragh in Kildare, ready to awaken to defend Ireland if the need arises. Clearly he's been slumbering too deeply as the need has arisen about a gazillion times in subsequent centuries and still no sign of Gerry and ghostly feckin' army.

SILKEN THOMAS

(1503–1537)

His trendy nickname, along with his disastrous uprising, earned Silken Thomas a prominent place in Irish history, although in retrospect, he probably would have preferred lording about his Kildare estates into old age rather than having his young head removed from his shoulders.

He was the grandson of Garret the Great, the 8th Earl of Kildare (P64), and by his time Henry VIII had his arse on the throne and was beheading and torturing the bejaysus out of anyone who didn't recognise him as head of the church instead of the pope. In February 1534, his beady eye came to rest on Silken Thomas's father, Gerard, a Catholic, who was summoned to London. Gerard appointed Thomas, then 31, as the Deputy Governor of Ireland in his absence, expecting to be back in time to see the first daffs sprouting, but little realising he'd soon be pushing up daisies himself.

In England, Gerard was given accommodation in the Tower of London, awaiting trial for some makey-

uppy charges. Unfortunately in June, a rumour reached Ireland that he'd been executed. When Thomas heard, he was fit to be tied. He gathered 140 horse-men, all of whom wore fancy silk fringes or ribbons on their helmets, thus the nickname, and they rode like blue-arsed flies to St. Mary's Abbey in Dublin (where Abbey Street gets its name). Here Thomas dramatically flung down his sword of state in front of the Council and renounced his allegiance to Henry. Bad idea.

Thomas tried to lay siege to Dublin Castle but used canons that were too light to breach the fortifications, and killed lots of ordinary Dubs, who turned on Thomas's forces. Worse was to come. A prominent archbishop, John Allen, who was taking refuge within the walls, decided to leg it, escaping through the underground Poddle River to the Liffey. But his escape was up the Swanee when he ran aground and was captured. Thomas is said to have ordered his supporters to put him in custody, but 'put him in custody' was somehow misinterpreted as 'hack him into gobbets'. As a result the entire church turned against the uprising.

Having failed to take Dublin Castle, the rebellion turned northwards. Thomas's supporters hacked their way from Dublin to Drogheda, butchering everyone suspected of supporting the Crown.

No, I did not say to go and 'Bash the Bishop'

Henry VIII dispatched a guy called William Skeffington, a nasty piece of wo it out. Among other things, ington is credited with the invention of the 'Scavenger's Daughter', torture device that basically squashed the body parts together until blood exploded from the head. Clearly a lovely chap. Skeffington sorted out

Whoarrr... Scavenger's Daughter

71

the Irish problem alright, first by plundering and murdering his way through all of the FitzGerald lands in Kildare. Thomas was away from his gaff, Maynooth Castle, looking for reinforcements when Skeffington attacked in March 1535, and after a bloody battle, the inhabitants sought terms for surrender, which were granted. Skeffington, having promised mercy, then executed the survivors. What a geebag.

Skeffington dropped dead later that year, thank feck, but his replacement was almost as treacherous. Lord Leonard Grey arrived and pursued Thomas to his refuge in the south. He offered Thomas and his supporters a promise of clemency. Thomas accepted and, of course, Grey immediately packed him off to the Tower of London. Jaysus, will we ever learn?

Thomas lingered in filth for 18 months, his misery evident from a letter he wrote:

'I never had money since I came into prison, and I have gone shirtless, barefoot and barelegged divers times, and should have died still, but that other poor prisoners hath sometimes given me old clothing.'

Long gone were the days of fancy silk scarves. In February 1537, he and his five uncles were '...draune from the Tower in to Tyborne, and there alle hongyd and hedded and quartered.'

You have to credit Silken Thomas for having a go. Unfortunately his efforts had the opposite effect, as Henry VIII decided to pay Ireland more attention i.e. batter the crap out of us more often. In the centuries after Thomas's rebellion, the English Crown strengthened their grip so much, that the whole country nearly choked to death.

GRACE O'MALLEY

(1530–1603)

Thanks to the attitudes of the time, most of the ladies of Irish history played a bit part, usually being married off to some head-the-ball to form an alliance or something. But not Grace O'Malley, otherwise known as Gráinne O'Malley, otherwise known as Granuaile, otherwise known as 'The Pirate Queen.'

Born into a seafaring family in Murrisk on the Mayo coast, her father Dubhdara O'Máille wasn't short of a few bob, being an O'Malley clan chieftain with an international trading business. Grace had saltwater in her veins from day one and, as a young cailín, asked her father to take her to Spain, but he refused because her long hair would get caught in the rigging, so she promptly cut it all off, earning her the nickname 'Gráinne Mhaol' (pronounced Grawn-neh-whale), or 'Baldy Gráinne'.

At 16 she was married off in a political alliance to Donal 'Of the Battles' O'Flaherty, who surprise, surprise was a belligerent sort. It seemed Grace was destined to live in a man's shadow. She produced three snappers with Donal, Owen, Murrough and Margaret, before Donal engaged in one clan dispute too many and was killed in 1560.

Now 30, Grace hadn't spent her youth changing nappies, but sailing the seven seas, roaring orders at sailors and generally kicking arse. By the time Donal met the grim reaper, she'd earned the respect of his soldiers who would gladly follow her as she fearlessly charged into battle. One of her earliest conflicts was when she re-took one of her dead husband's castles, called Cock Castle, from the Joyce clan, leading the Joyces to rename it 'Hen's Castle' (the name still stands). English soldiers once attacked the castle and legend recounts that she had the castle's lead roof melted and poured down on the soldiers' heads. Ouch. Not surprisingly, they fled like scalded cats.

Around 1564, she decided to take up residence on Clare Island and her small army duly followed her. From here she started 'taxing' passing boats. Her ships pursued any vessel unlucky to come within sight, and demanded payment. If this was refused, well, you'd find a sword suddenly protruding from your bellybutton. This behaviour brought her to the Crown's attention.

Around this time Grace's ship rescued a youth called Hugh de Lacy from drowning, and Grace took a fancy to him. To young Hugh, Grace was probably a sixteenth-century version of a rich, well-preserved cougar. Sadly the love-story didn't have a happy ending, as they'd barely had time for some hanky panky below decks when Hugh was killed by the Mac-Mahon clan. Hell hath no fury like a woman robbed of her toy boy, so Grace attacked the MacMahons while they were on pilgrimage, butchered those responsible, captured their ships and seized their castle. You really didn't want to mess with this lady.

The following year she married a guy called Richard-in-Iron Bourke, because his castle was more defensible than hers. Although it was supposedly a political arrangement, Richard would later come to her rescue, so he must have had a soft spot in his iron for her. She also bore him a son, Theobald.

Over the years, Grace continued to attack ships around the coast and once fended off the infamous Barbary pirates. She even launched raids on castles along the shoreline. Her reputation as a leader and military tactician left the élite gobsmacked. How could a mere slip of a woman command such fear and respect?

In 1576, Grace's ship was off Howth, north of Dublin, when she decided to pay a courtesy visit to Baron Howth, but was informed that the family was dining, and didn't wish to be disturbed. Deeply offended, Grace replied by kidnapping the Baron's grandson, and only released him when a pledge was given that the gates of the castle always be kept open for unexpected visitors and an extra place set at every meal – the arrangement is still honoured by the descendants of the Baron, in case Grace's ghost drops in for some take-away Egg Foo Yung.

But it wasn't all plain sailing. Within months of this she was captured while raiding the Desmond area in Munster and eventually thrown into Dublin Castle's dungeons. The hubby, Richard, who'd been quietly living in the missus's shadow, raised a rebellion and the English thought, 'Oh, for f**k's sake, holding this woman is more trouble than it's worth', so they duly released her. Big mistake, as Grace then raided English ships left, right and centre and even repelled the army that besieged her in Rockfleet castle.

A few years later Richard cashed in his chips and, around the same time, a gouger called Sir Richard Bingham was appointed Governor of Connaught.

He was determined to see the back of Grace, who was now supporting Irish rebel lords. Bingham would later describe her to Queen Elizabeth I as the 'nurse to all rebellions in the province for this 40 years'. Among other things he had her son, Owen, killed, and her other son, Theobald, arrested, and charged Grace herself with treason. He launched attack after attack and destroyed most of Grace's fleet, and for the first time in her life, the Pirate Queen was on the back foot.

But she wasn't done yet. She wrote to the Queen and asked for an audience. And in 1593, at the age of 63, she arrived in the court of Elizabeth I. She might easily have had her head separated from her shoulders, but clearly oul' Lizzy believed she'd found a kindred spirit – a woman who could kick arse with the best of them. The pair spent hours gossiping in Latin about the latest fashions in torture devices and the general uselessness of men, until Lizzy agreed not only to have Grace's son released but also to give Bingham the boot. In return Grace agreed to stop supporting rebellions by Irish lords against the Crown.

Back home, the deal was partly honoured, with Bingham at least temporarily removed. But Grace's lands were not returned, so sure enough she returned to pirating, and the ould bat was still at the helm yelling at sailors when she was a sprightly 67.

I love your wooden teeth.

But time and tide eventually caught up with even Grace, and she finally hauled anchor and set sail for Heaven around 1603, in her early seventies. By then she'd achieved legendary status and her life is remembered in a gansey-load of songs, Broadway shows, novels, monuments, exhibitions etc. She was a woman ahead of her time, even if she spent lots of that time robbing stuff that wasn't hers!

HUGH O'NEILL

(1550–1616)

One of the worst things about learning Irish history in school was the depressing number of times we heard of Irish armies getting the shite kicked out of them by the English. Hugh O'Neill, aka The Great Earl, at least gave us a brief respite from this gloom, having turned the tables more than once on the ould enemy. Ultimately, it would all end in failure, but for a while there was a brief glimmer...

Hugh wasn't always the rebel. Although born into the powerful Ulster O'Neill clan, he grew up in the Pale, surrounded by snooty Anglo-Irish types, having being banished there when his father was killed in a clan dispute. He returned to Ulster, aged 18, all hormones and ambition, determined to get back his grandfather's title of Earl of Tyrone, and happy to accept help from the Crown. In reality Queen Liz and her cronies wanted to use O'Neill and other Irish lords as puppets to help them subjugate Ireland. Eventually, after helping the English to suppress a few minor rebellions, he was granted the title in 1587.

But O'Neill had other plans beyond having some poncy English title, because the real power lay in the position of The O'Neill, i.e. recognised as the head honcho by every O'Neill on the planet. Unfortunately there was no vacancy, as Turlough Luineach O'Neill held the position, who wasn't in the Crown's good books. So Hugh was again happy to accept their help in overcoming him, and after about a gazillion litres of blood had been spilled, in 1593 Turlough abdicated and went for a few pints instead.

But, having reached the top in Ulster, Hugh decided he wanted it all for himself, without having to answer to some oul' wagon in England. He asked the Spanish for help and, Jaysus, were they slow. So the English sent a large force under Sir John Norris to knock Hugh back into line. But in 1595 Hugh's forces attacked the Blackwater Fort in Armagh and chopped up its English soldiers, destroyed the fort and got the feck out of there. Norris declared O'Neill a traitor. There was no going back now.

The English thought it would only be a matter of time before they'd sort out this cheeky Irish upstart. It *was* a matter of time – nine years worth of it. They'd failed to realise how cute a cute hoor Hugh was. He'd made an alliance with Ulster's other powerful clan, the O'Donnells, led by Red Hugh O'Donnell (P86). He'd also been training the ordinary Joe Soaps, and the Spanish sent a load of gunpowder and guns. Hugh handed his first significant arse-kicking to the English, when his forces ambushed an English force at Clontibret in Monaghan and wiped out nearly half of them. He then decided to call a halt while he waited for Spanish reinforcements.

By the way, in the time before, during and after the Nine Years War, Hugh managed to marry four women and to get innumerable mistresses into the sack. But as The O'Neill you just had to look sideways at a woman and she'd agree to bear your children. Hugh fathered eight legitimate snappers and loads of little bastards, as they were affectionately known.

Not counting his bedroom antics, his next close encounter

The Hugh O'Neill effect

would be a famous one in 1598, at the Battle of Yellow Ford in Armagh. His forces battered the bejaysus out of a large English army led by Sir Henry Bagenal, who earned himself a bullet in the head. The defeat was one of the biggest ever of an English army in Ireland and it united most of the other clan chiefs around the country, who all immediately decided it might be wise to support Hugh. He was proclaimed High King of Ireland. Was there any stopping the man?

Queen Liz was like a mad yoke and dispatched the Earl of Essex to Ireland with 17,000 men. Essex fluthered about around the south for a few months, winning the occasional skirmish but suffering some major defeats, especially at the Battle of Curlew Pass (by O'Neill's ally Red Hugh O'Donnell), until finally deciding to head north and face O'Neill. News of Essex's ineffectiveness reaching the queen, it was reported that she 'stamped with her feet and thrust her rusty sword at times into her arras in great rage.' Sounds painful, but luckily her arras was a type of tapestry. Essex reached the battleground up north, saw the size of O'Neill's forces and thought 'Oh shit!' A conference was called at which O'Neill won very generous terms,

Elizabeth I and her stitched up arras

so generous that Essex returned to England with his tail between his legs. A couple of years later his head was between his legs as well – beheaded for treason.

Finally, in 1601, only six years late, 4000 Spanish soldiers arrived. Unfortunately they were as useless as tits on a bull. Firstly they landed at Kinsale, the wrong end of the country, and then they allowed themselves to be besieged by English forces before they'd even had time to whip up a few tapas dishes. With winter approaching, O'Neill and O'Donnell headed south to support the Spanish, but they ran short of supplies so resorted to plunder. Of course, this lost them a lot of support and by the time they reached Kinsale their army was pretty banjaxed. In addition, O'Neill's forces were used to ambushing the enemy and then legging it, so when they came up against a large English force in open conflict, they were totally outmatched and were left minus lots of heads, arms, legs etc. The Spanish surrendered and were allowed to return to sunny Spain with their castanets still intact.

O'Neill retreated north and continued to resist with a few skirmishes, but the fight had been knocked out of him. In 1603, Queen Liz decided to offer peace terms, which were completed just six days after her death. Her successor, King James I, allowed Hugh to keep most of his lands, but the old earl couldn't take the loss of power and status, and decided to make tracks out of Ireland. In 1607, he and about 100 other chieftains, along with the missuses and loads of bawling kids, embarked on a ship for Spain. This was the momentous event in Irish history called The Flight of the Earls, marking the end of the ancient Gaelic order.

Poor Hugh never made it to Spain, though he did reach Rome, where he had a Papal audience with

Pope Paul V, so at least he had something to stick in the photo album. He spent his final years plotting in vain to return and finally bate the English back across the Irish sea, but he finally gave up the ghost on July 20th 1616.

Shame really. A bit of luck here, a small change of plans there, and it all might have been so different. But *que sera sera*. We were stuck with the Sassanachs for another 300 years.

RED HUGH O'DONNELL

(1572–1602)

~

Red Hugh O'Donnell (aka Aodh Ruadh Ó Domhnaill) presumably got the 'Red' nickname because he was a coppertop, but by the time he was a pimply teenager he had reason enough to see red as well.

His father was the powerful Hugh, King of Tír Chonaill (Donegal). Fearful of an alliance between the O'Donnells and the O'Neills, the Lord Deputy of Ireland, Sir John Perrot, a right sleeveen by all accounts, kidnapped 15 year old Hugh and threw him into Dublin Castle's dungeons, where he would remain as a hostage for five years. His escape in 1592 would earn him a place in the top 10 anecdotes of Irish history, as no one had ever escaped the castle.

Somehow knocking their shackles off, he and two fellow prisoners of the O'Neill clan, Art and Henry, knotted a rope and climbed down into the prison jacks, then via the sewers, into the castle moat. They'd deliberately chosen a bitter cold night so that  the sentries would be more worried about freezing their nuts off than watching for escapees. They were met by a boy sent to help by Hugh O'Neill, and he guided them out of the city. The trio then proceeded to cross the Dublin/Wicklow mountains in a snow-storm, headed for the secret mountain hideout of an ally, Fiach MacHugh O'Byrne at Glenmalure, on the other side of the mountains. It was a monumental journey, undertaken without proper clothes, shoes or food. Art didn't make it, but the others struggled on and reached the lair after several days, although Red Hugh was minus two toes. There's a plaque near the spot where Art fell and an annual walk follows their footsteps, although the guys nowadays are all wearing thermal underwear, electrically heated boots and iPods.

Back in Donegal, his father abdicated leaving Red Hugh as chieftain, aged just 20. His first act was to rid the county of its murderous gouger of a sheriff and pals, and those he didn't run out, he ran through. He then joined forces with Hugh O'Neill (P80) in the Nine Years War. He seized control of the area from Sligo to Leitrim and then battered the English at the Battle of Clontibret in 1595. The dynamic duo went one better

Great Irish victories

a few years later, hockeying the English at the Battle of Yellow Ford.

But O'Donnell's later plundering of Galway for supplies was one of his few bad moves, as robbing all someone's cattle and crops won't really win their hearts, and his forces ravaging all over Connaught lost him much of the support of the local chieftains.

In 1599, Red Hugh's army ambushed English forces under Sir Conyers Clifford as they passed through the Curlew Mountains in Roscommon. Clifford and about 600 of his men bit the bog; Red Hugh's casualties roughly amounted to two sprained wrists and a cut or two that needed a Band Aid.

Then came the big showdown, when Hugh marched his forces south to engage the English at Kinsale. He'd had good practice of long, freezing cold walks of course, but this was something else. To make sure they didn't miss the fun, his army marched 40 miles a day across mountains, bogs and rivers in the depths of winter. Unfortunately when they reached the battle they were all completely knackered. The young, rash, Red Hugh insisted on an immediate attack, whereas the more cautious O'Neill wanted his army to have a bit of R&R before they rushed to their deaths. Anyway, the battle went badly, and their army was routed.

While Hugh O'Neill carried on the war for a while, Red Hugh decided to leg it to Spain and try to rally support personally from King Phillip III. He sailed to Corunna in Galicia where he was treated like a king himself. The place was home to Irish chieftains who'd already fled, and a right old hooley was had. He eventually managed to get a promise of support from Phillip, but as previously, it was slow to materialise, and while waiting he caught a fever and died at the age of just 30. Dark rumours abounded that Red Hugh was poisoned by an English agent, James Blake, and there is evidence that it might well be true. Which just goes to show how worried Queen Lizzie was about the charismatic Red Hugh, and the influence he might have had on his Spanish royal hosts. Pity he died so young, because who knows, he might have gotten the army he wanted and led an invasion of Ireland, and we'd all be speaking Spanish now.

He was buried at Simancas Castle in central Spain and a plaque there honours his memory. Red Hugh was also the subject of a 1966 Walt Disney movie, *The Fighting Prince of Donegal*, in which all the characters said things like 'Well, top o' the morning te ye, let's go and kill some English feckers, be de hokey.'

OWEN ROE O'NEILL

(C. 1585–1649)

Another famous O'Neill, Owen was among the greatest in terms of military leadership, and is renowned for perhaps one of the greatest Irish victories in history. Jaysus, he gave the enemy a right batin' that day.

His father was Art O'Neill, a brother of the Great Earl, Hugh O'Neill (P80), so given his bloodline, he was probably rarin' to spill English guts before he was out of his sheepskin nappies.

He served with his father and uncle in the Nine Years War, but his clan were forced to skedaddle abroad in The Flight of the Earls. Owen made the most of his exile however, and shot up the ranks of the Spanish Irish regiment faster than a greyhound on a greasy surface with a firework up its arse. He earned particular renown for commanding the garrison during the Siege of Arras, when he held out with 2000 men for months against 30,000 Frenchmen. This guy clearly knew his stuff and would definitely come in handy back home.

The Roe O'Neills, a family portrait

In between pouring buckets of boiling water on French people, he married Rosa O'Dogherty, and they had one son. It was said, however, that Owen also had a moxy load of illegitimate snappers, probably because he was a dashing, good-looking general who had killed loads of French guys, and that was the sort of thing that really turned on Spanish ladies.

Owen spent 30 years in the Spanish Army, all the while wishing that the French and Dutch he was disembowelling were English. When the Confederate Wars broke out in Ireland in 1641, he gathered 300 veterans and sailed home to Donegal.

What had happened back on the ould sod was that a mostly bloodless coup was planned by Phelim O'Neill, Owen's cousin, but the plan was banjaxed when the Ulster Irish rose up against the English and Scottish settlers and basically butchered loads of them, men, women and children. The rebellion spread and in 1642, a Confederation of Irish Catholic nobles, clergy and soldiers convened in Kilkenny to organise the war effort, thus the name. Civil war had just broken out in England, and many of the confederates supported the Royalist forces of Charles I and would have been happy to remain under the Crown if they got certain powers. Owen had other ideas. He simply wanted the English out of Ireland and didn't give a crap about Charles I.

Owen Roe was welcomed with open arms, and after a while Phelim O'Neill resigned command in favour of Owen. After some early setbacks, the Papal Nuncio, Archbishop Rinuccini, doing God's work, arrived with loads of weapons and gunpowder, courtesy of the Pope, and things started looking up. The

Did I say arms? I meant alms.

saintly Rinuccini was keen to kick out as many Protestants as possible and leave Ireland free to govern itself. Unfortunately neither man got on well with the Confederation, particularly the fact that some of them supported Charles I. On top of that, Owen was rightly miffed that the Confederation was giving most of its military support to the Leinster army of Thomas Preston, another veteran of the Spanish army. Owen Roe and Preston hated each others' guts.

But his day in the sun was at hand. A large English-backed army of Scottish Covenanters landed in Ireland in 1646 under the command of Robert Munro. Owen Roe met at them at Benburb in Tyrone on the banks of the Blackwater, and it was here that his tactical genius came into play. He'd thoroughly disciplined his men and armed them with longer-shafted pikes than was standard. He positioned his army on the higher ground and also manoeuvred Munroe's army so their backs were to the river. Strategically, he was one cute hoor. The longer pikes allowed his men to basically skewer lots of poor Scots, as their weapons couldn't reach the Irish lads. Munro's army panicked and was driven back into a bend in the river, and those not disembow- elled, drowned trying to escape. All in all, Munro's army lost almost half its number – 3000 men. So it was drinks all round that night for the Irish lads.

Unfortunately, they man- aged to royally screw things up for themselves as, due to infighting in the Confederation, they failed to take advantage of the victory. They did agree to launch an assault on Dublin, but instead of giving Owen Roe command, they made him share it with Thomas Preston, and as pointed out earlier, Owen believed that Preston was as useful as a concrete currach. Sure enough, too many cooks spoiled the attack and they were forced to retreat.

Confederation forces suffered several defeats in the following years, including the slaughter of Pres- ton's army at the Battle of Dungan's Hill in Meath in

1647, and eventually were forced to negotiate with the Royalists, infuriating Owen Roe and Rinuccini, who decided to get his arse back to Rome. Owen Roe was left isolated, his army disheartened. In desperation, he agreed to ally his forces with the Confederation again, even though they'd signed a pact pledging allegiance to Charles I. Cromwell, the murderous oul' bollox, arrived in Ireland in August of that same year, 1649.

Owen Roe would never have the chance to pit his tactical skill against the murderous bowsie, as he became ill in November and died at Cloughoughter Castle in Cavan. The place of his burial is unknown.

With his death, the Confederation lost its most gifted military leader, and Cromwell's forces went on a rampage, ultimately resulting in up to a quarter of a million deaths. But that's another story.

Not exactly a happy ending. Two centuries later he was commemorated in a famous song written by Thomas Davis (P186), called 'The Lament for Owen Roe'. The last verse sums it all up:

Soft as woman's was your voice, O'Neill! bright was your eye,

O! why did you leave us, Eoghan? Why did you die?
Your troubles are all over, you're at rest with God on high,
But we're slaves, and we're orphans, Eoghan! Why did you die?

ST. OLIVER PLUNKETT

(1625–1681)

～

In 1975, Oliver Plunkett became our first official new saint since Lawrence O'Toole, about seven centuries earlier. This roughly equates with our success rate at international soccer tournaments.

Born in 1625 in Loughcrew, Meath, Olly was from a family who could afford to educate him, and he was soon earmarked for the priesthood, which was considered the height of career success back then. He was sent to Rome in 1647 and his timing couldn't have been better, as a couple of years later Cromwell and pals started hanging/burning/impaling priests and bishops. Not surprisingly, Olly wouldn't be back for a while.

He was ordained in 1654 but unable to go home, he spent a lot of time reflecting on religious stuff, and became a professor of theology. And then in 1669, aged 44, he was appointed Archbishop of Armagh and Primate of All Ireland. This took a good few people aback, as he'd spent most of his adult life wandering the Vatican communing with God and hadn't a single day's pastoral experience, i.e. he'd never been out in the field, as such. But Olly certainly threw himself in at the deep end, returning to the auld sod the following year. By then Charles II was the bigwig on the throne, and was too busy showing youngwans his royal sceptre (he fathered at least 12 children by almost as many mistresses) to bother about serious Catholic repression.

Oliver's first job when he arrived back was to sort out his own priests, who it seems had been on one massive bender for years. He wrote: 'Let us remove this defect [the drink] from an Irish priest, and he will be a saint'. The booze mopped up, he turned to educating us ignorant galoots and set up a Jesuit

College in Drogheda. He was a big hit with locals starved of spiritual sustenance, and in four years, Oliver Plunkett confirmed almost 50,000 new Catholics.

But then things turned bad when, in 1672, the new Viceroy for Ireland, the Earl of Essex, banned all Catholic education and exiled all clergy. What a scumbag. Many bishops legged it, and the newly built college in Drogheda, was flattened. But Olly decided to stay and spent years wandering the country in disguise, ministering to his flock on mountainsides.

If all that wasn't bad enough, things turned decidedly worse in 1678, with the 'Popish Plot' came to light. This was a complete fiction created by a Catholic-hating English fruitcake called Titus Oates, and supposedly involved a Papal-inspired plot to assassinate Charles II. This would ultimately result in the execution of 15 innocent men and a frenzy of

Titus, you're a lying perjuring villain. So please accept this generous pension.

anti-Catholicism in Britain and Ireland. The English finally captured Oliver Plunkett in Dublin in 1679. He was later tried in Drogheda for plotting to bring a French invasion into Ireland and raising rebellion. The charges were, of course, as fabricated as a TD's expenses claim.

Despite the fact that the entire jury were Protestants, the powers-that-be realised they wouldn't get a conviction in Ireland, as Olly was too well-liked. So they moved the trial to London, threw him in the slammer for months, and spent the time organising a kangaroo court. He was denied a proper defence and the prosecution witnesses were a bunch of criminal gougers. The judge, Lord Pemberton, was the biggest scumbag of all, repeatedly frustrating Oliver's attempts to defend himself. The jury took just 15

minutes to find him guilty and Pemberton ruled that Oliver 'be given a brutal death, befitting a traitor,' and sentenced him to be hanged, drawn and quartered. Oliver Plunkett replied 'Thanks be to God.'

He was taken to Tyburn for execution on July 1st 1681, where, from the scaffold he publicly forgave all those responsible – saintly indeed, as most people would want to rip their guts out. The details of the execution would probably turn you off your lunch. Afterwards, various bits of him went to different places as everyone wanted a souvenir. His head travelled to Rome, then Armagh, and finally ended up in St. Peter's Church, Drogheda, where you can still have a morbid peek at it. Most of his body was buried in England but various other bits are in France, Australia, Germany and America.

Oliver Plunkett was the last Catholic martyr to die in England. He was beatified in 1920 and canonised in 1975.

ROBERT BOYLE

(1627–1691)

~

We're not exactly rolling in famous scientists here, but can claim one of most renowned of the lot – Waterford man Robert Boyle was one of the founders of modern chemistry, and he truly was a gas man.

Born rolling in spondulicks, his father was the 1st Earl of Cork, and they lived on a vast estate, called Lismore Castle, nicked from the native Irish. But he did mix with the locals and could actually speak Irish, which is more than you can say for most Irish people. He was a clever little brat, and his father packed him off to Eton and then Europe for further education. He later related some experiences he had in Europe, one involving two manky oul' friars trying to have their wicked way with him, who he called 'gowned sod-omites'. And he experienced a violent thunderstorm that he thought would kill him, and which turned him into a religious nut. He also developed a fascination with how the world worked and when he returned to England in 1644 he devoted his life to science and to God. Early on he developed his technique of analysis through experiment and observation, as opposed to general speculation, also known as talking though your arse.

When he was 20 he started coming home to Ireland to run his deceased father's estates, but became very frustrated as it was hard to find a decent elliptical elixir distilling apparatus anywhere. So after a few years he returned to Oxford and started bonding with the élite scientific clique. He was fascinated by the behaviour of gas, especially if he'd eaten baked beans the night before, and he experimented relentlessly with air, discovering many of its characteristics, such as its role in combustion, breathing and transmitting sound. He also discovered the relationship between the pressure of a gas and its volume, which you might remember from school if you were paying attention, called Boyle's Law. By now he was one of the most renowned boffins of the age. He even formulated a theory that all matter was made of

very, very, very, small bits differentiated by shape and motion, which essentially turned out to be true.

Robert also had a scientific wish list that included figuring out how to have eternal life, flying, breathing underwater and the development of a drug that would 'Exalt Imagination, Waking, Memory, and other Functions, and appease Pain, procure innocent Sleep', which sounds like a druggie's dream. Most of his wish list came true, although scientists have yet to crack the eternal life thing (please hurry up). He did, unfortunately, also dabble in alchemy, his attempts to turn lead into gold leaving the only blot on his scientific notebook.

Robert was a devout Christian and figured that a better scientific understanding of the universe would bring him closer to God. What inevitably did bring him a lot closer to God, however, was his death in London on New Year's Eve 1691, at the age of 64.

PATRICK SARSFIELD

(1660–1693)

A Lucan lad, Patrick Sarsfield would ultimately distinguish himself in Limerick, where he had a victorious defeat, if such a thing is possible.

Born in 1660 into a posh Catholic family, Patrick already had some pedigree in slugging it out with the English, as his grandfather Rory O'More was a leader in the 1641 uprising. He had a few interesting experiences as a young gentleman, including getting run through with a sword while acting as a second in a duel – he obviously didn't stand back far enough. And he had some strange incidents with ladies, first when he helped a pal to abduct a wealthy widow who the pal wanted to marry. This sort of thing went on then – a chap fancied a girl who wouldn't return his advances, so bob's your uncle, he simply imprisoned her until she changed her mind. Mind you, it was illegal. Anyway, clearly not learning from this experience, he attempted to kidnap his own bride, one Elizabeth Herbert. But Lizzy stood her ground,

Fancy me yet?

Nope.

and refused to marry Patrick, promising not to prosecute him if he released her, which he duly did.

Presumably he grew out of spouse-kidnapping, as we all do, and went on to become a soldier, seeing action in France and England, and becoming a colonel. While in France, he met the future King James II, who was in temporary exile, and the pair got on like a house on fire, although James thought Patrick was a bit of a bonehead, calling him 'a brave fellow, but very scantily supplied with brains.' Look who's talking. Anyway, he later promoted Patrick to major-general and one of the chief honchos appointed to make the army in Ireland a Catholic-dominated one.

In 1688, Patrick's elder brother kicked the bucket and he found himself the principal heir. He also found himself a wife, Honora Burke, and he didn't even have to kidnap her. Then along came the Williamite War, and Patrick's chance to strut his stuff.

Initially it went well and in the first months of the war he took control of Connaught for the Jacobites

(Catholic supporters of James). But then James and his army had their arses seriously kicked at the Battle of the Boyne and the Battle of Aughrim, where Patrick fought a valiant rearguard action, yet became acquainted with most of his men's innards. James legged it to France, earning him the nickname in Ireland of 'Seamus an Chaca'. For those with just the cúpla focal, that's 'James the Shit'.

Conversely, Patrick was described as 'a gentleman of eminent merit, brave, upright, honourable, careful of his men in quarters, and always found at their head in battle.' And those leadership qualities allowed him to rally the remnants of his army at Limerick, where they would make one final stand against the nasty Williamites.

Sure enough old Billy's army turned up with about 40,000 dudes, and as Patrick's army behind the walls was about a third of that number, the English expected a walkover. One of the Jacobite commanders in Limerick was a French geezer called Lauzun, who wanted to surrender. But our Paddy was having none of it and rallied his troops to defend the walls. Then on August 9th, a couple of days after William arrived, he learned that the enemy's field artillery was still en-route from Dublin, and he snuck out of the city with 500 men. Guided by a man called Galloping Hogan, who would later win loads of medals in the Portuguese army, they intercepted William's guns at a place called Ballyneety, beat the bejaysus out of the soldiers and captured the lot, then headed back to the city.

William was mightily pissed off, as by the time he got replacement weapons, summer was on the wane, so he ordered an assault. They breached the outer wall, but a French engineer called Boiseleau had brilliantly engineered an inner wall of earth, and the Williamite forces found themselves trapped. To Patrick's Jacobite army, it was like shooting fish in a barrel, and the women, who'd stayed behind to support their men, did their bit by battering the poor feckers from above with rocks. All in all, the enemy lost 3000 men to a few hundred Jacobites. William's army was forced to retreat for the winter, and he decided to head back to the Netherlands, probably to get stoned out of his box.

Unfortunately William's army returned the following year, this time better prepared. They bombarded the walls and made a surprise attack on Thomond Bridge, outside the walls, forcing the Jacobites there to flee to the city gates. But the French Jacobite soldiers inside refused to open the gates, and nearly 1000 men were slaughtered. This would be the lowest ebb of Franco-Irish relations until Thierry Henry cheated in the world cup play-off in 2009. Patrick Sarsfield now knew the game was up and opened negotiations to surrender with the Williamite commander De Ginkell.

And he proved to be a good negotiator, as the Treaty of Limerick allowed the survivors to leave Ireland unharmed, or else stay and have their religious and property rights protected. Over 1400 opted to leave, in what became known as 'The Flight of the

Wild Geese'. Afterwards, the Williamite gougers conveniently forgot the bit about property and religious rights, and Ireland suffered one of its worst eras of persecution.

Poor Paddy Sarsfield took a ship to France and resumed his military career and sadly, a couple of years later, aged just 33, was mortally wounded in battle in Belgium. Famously, he is reputed to have looked at the blood pouring from his wound and said: 'Oh, if only this were for Ireland.'

Naturally he is still a big hit in Limerick, where he has various bridges, streets, buildings, statues, GAA clubs etc. in his honour. He even has a town in Canada named after him. Work that one out.

JONATHAN SWIFT

(1667–1745)

Leaving matters political, religious and societal, we turn to the life and work of Jonathan Swift, who spent much of his time slagging the hell out of matters political, religious and societal.

The greatest prose satirist in the English language was born in Dublin soon after his father unexpectedly popped his clogs. His mother, Abigail, offloaded the screaming mite to his uncle Godwin, who essentially raised him, sending him to a fine school in Kilkenny and then to Trinity. But the teenage Jonathan wasn't the brightest penny in the purse, and was only awarded his BA by 'speciali gratia', i.e. as a favour.

The political and religious upheavals in Ireland made Jonathan a bit nervy, so off he went to a friend of Uncle Goddy, Sir William Temple, in Surrey, whose huge library was like an Aladdin's Cave to young Jonathan. While there he also met the eight year old Esther Johnson, the daughter of a companion of Temple. He nicknamed her 'Stella' (he had a thing for nicknaming ladies) and they'd have a lifelong relationship. He returned to Ireland only a couple of times over the next decade, once to take holy orders in the Anglican Church.

While in Temple's home Jonathan dabbled unsuccessfully in writing poetry, but before long he'd turned his deft hand to satirical prose and found his calling. In 1694 his religious duties took him to rural Antrim, which he hated, but did have one distraction in a young lady called Jane Waring (whom he nick-named 'Varina'). Sadly she spurned his love and he went back to England until 1699. Around this time, he wrote *A Tale of a Tub*, which took the mick out of religious practices of the time.

Another church posting took him to Trim, Co. Meath, and a congregation of 15. Bored silly by 1702, he returned to England, where he hoped for a senior church appointment, but he'd upset Queen Anne with *A Tale of a Tub* and so was posted back to Ireland as Dean of St. Patrick's Cathedral. He was furious initially but it was to prove the making of him. To console himself, he reacquainted himself with Esther 'Stella' Johnson, now a big girl of 20. Their relationship would leave later scholars scratching their heads, as they never married, although some claimed they had married in secret. But undoubtedly the pair were head over heels in love.

Over the next 20 years, Jonathan's creative output spiralled upwards like the staircase in his cathedral (which he actually used to jog up and down to stay fit – fair fecks to him). He produced political pamphlets and works of satire that earned him the public's praise and the Government's and gentry's rage. Among his

Who put this in the cookery section?

works were *A Proposal for Universal Use of Irish Man-ufacture*, *Drapier's Letters* and *A Modest Proposal* – a brilliantly dark satire on the attitude of Dublin's rich towards the poor. In it, he proposes, straight-faced, that poor people's babies should be used as food to feed the rich. He writes: 'I have been assured…that a young healthy child is a most delicious, nourishing and wholesome food…'

He was by now regarded as a great, beloved Irish patriot, particularly for his work with the poor; he gave half his annual salary away to needy causes. He blamed the poverty in Ireland on the misadministra-tion of the English Government and they tried to shut him up a few times. Yet his work continued to make them a laughing stock.

On a trip to London in 1709 he'd met another lady called Esther Vanhomrigh (who he nicknamed 'Vanessa') and, while it is not known how he felt about her, it is known that she was besotted with him, even following him to Dublin. Jonathan, probably thinking that Stella might throw a wobbly, tried but failed to dissuade her. Eventually however poor Vanessa got the boot and Stella remained his one true love until she died, leaving him heartbroken, in 1728.

In the 1720s, he produced his masterpiece, known to most of the world as *Gulliver's Travels*, but known to the literati by its original title: *Travels into Several Remote Nations of the World, in Four Parts, by Lemuel Gulliver, First a Surgeon, and then a Captain of Several Ships*. Snappy.

It's strange how many people believe it's a children's book, when it is, in fact, a scathing satire on politics, religion and humanity. It is full of the sharpest satire, like the silly acrobatics that characters perform to get elected, or crazy scientists performing experiments such as trying to turn shite back into food (a pop at several English scientific institutions). It also made brilliant but caustic observations about humanity, such as when Gulliver lands on an island inhabited by the near-perfect Houyhnhnms and the brutal, filthy Yahoos, which also gave the

word to the English language. The book has been in print since 1726.

In his last years Jonathan went a bit wonky in the head. He used to pick quarrels and yell at anyone who glanced sideways at him. He became unsteady on his feet and small noises irritated him. At one point his eye swelled to the size of an egg and it took five people to stop him ripping it out. Jonathan finally kicked the bucket in 1745 and was buried in the cathedral alongside his Stella. A century later, Sir William Wilde (Oscar's Daddy), exhumed his body and discovered that poor Jonathan had been suffering from Meniere's Disease, which produce severe vertigo and makes small noises sound like explosions. The poor fecker. He left most of his fortune to found a hospital for the mentally ill, originally called St. Patrick's Hospital for Imbeciles, which still exists, although they dropped the 'imbeciles' bit.

Jonathan Swift liked to poke fun at politicians. With all the material he'd have to work with in Ireland nowadays, can you imagine the masterpieces he'd churn out, were he alive?

TURLOUGH O'CAROLAN

(1670–1738)

A brief musical interlude amid all the bloody clamour of Ireland's past. Often called 'Ireland's National Composer', in his day he was as big as Bono. Had sunglasses been available at the time he might even have worn them (but mainly because he went blind, as opposed to because of some pretentious wankology).

Turlough was born in 1670 in Nobber in County Meath. His father, a blacksmith, relocated the clan to Roscommon and took a job with the local toffs, the MacDermott-Roes. Mrs Mac realised Turlough showed great poetic potential and had him educated. But sadly Turlough caught smallpox as a teen, which left him blind, so the good lady then decided he'd have to use his ears to get through life and had him taught to play the harp.

Three years later, his generous patron provided Turlough with a horse, a guide, a harp and a wad of cash and sent him out into the big bad world. And it *was* a big bad world – Ireland was in chaos after the Battle of the Boyne and soon the Penal Laws would make life for Catholics really wojus.

Off he went on a journey around Ireland that would last 45 years, stopping at the castles and homes of posh people to entertain them with his musical skills. Actually, it was soon obvious that Turlough was a fairly average harpist, but when one patron, George Reynolds of Leitrim, suggested he try composing, the young man quickly found his own rhythm, and was soon churning out tunes by the cartload. Many of these became so famous that he started receiving invites to perform them from all over the country. He composed songs and instrumentals, and reputedly

117

invented the word 'planxty' – a song in honour of a patron. He became so revered that weddings and even funerals were often delayed for days until he could arrive. Fine enough if it was a wedding but if it was a funeral, in the days before refrigeration you'd be praying he'd arrive sooner rather than later.

He was living the life of Reilly, and was known to enjoy a drink or 10. At one point a doctor advised him to stop drinking to improve his health, but he ended up feeling worse, so found another doctor who gave him the opposite advice! He even composed a verse to celebrate the joys of booze:

He's a fool who give over the liquor,
It softens the skinflint at once,
It urges the slow coach on quicker,
Gives spirit and brains to the dunce.
The man who is dumb as a rule
Discovers a great deal to say,
While he who is bashful since Yule
Will talk in an amorous way.

A true Irishman – and in more ways than one. He was 50 before he got around to marrying Mary Maguire, but the two evidently harmonised well together as they produced seven kids. He continued to compose and perform until his late sixties, producing such famed works as *Carolan's Concerto*, *Carolan's Receipt* and *Carolan's Welcome*. Over 200 of his compositions survive. And despite the oppressive Penal Times, he frequently performed at secret, illegal masses.

He died in 1738 and was buried in Kilronan Cemetery, Roscommon, and 60 priests reputedly came out of hiding to officiate at his funeral. His work was popularised again by trad bands such as Planxty (yep, they got their name from Turlough), The Chief-

Oooh! I've found a Turlough!

tains and The Dubliners. There's a statue of Turlough in Nobber and a memorial in St. Pat's Cathedral, Dublin. He was depicted on the old £50 note and there's a harp of his in Clonalis House, Castlerea. Oh, and there's also a cream liqueur named after him – and a pound to a penny that's the honour he would have appreciated most of all.

GEORGE BERKELEY

(1685–1753)

One of the brainiest fellas ever born here, George was one of the great philosophers of his age. Ever seen *The Matrix*? Then you've come across some of his theories.

Born in Kilkenny of Anglo-Irish stock, he was smarter than his teachers and was soon heading for Trinners, aged just 15. He had his degree at 17 and

his masters at 22. He was a bit of a polymath; a philosopher, expert mathematician, spoke Greek, Latin and Hebrew, and had an interest in natural sciences, theology, science. Are you keeping up? No? Neither could anyone else.

The whiz kid published his first major work of philosophy at 24, called *An Essay Towards a New Theory of Vision*. This was soon followed by his most famous work: *A Treatise Concerning the Principle of Human Knowledge*. In case you fancy pondering your existence, his philosophical theory was called 'immaterialism' and it essentially says that matter only exists in the perceiver's mind, and without your brain to perceive stuff, it'd go 'poofff' and vanish. So this book doesn't really exist, so you might as well just go for a

The question is, Madam, are they for real?

pint. Except that, oh crap, the pint doesn't really exist either!

At 30 years old, George moved to London and was soon rubbing shoulders with all the other top-drawer philosophers, writers and politicians such as Jonathan Swift and Alexander Pope. After dazzling London and leaving them much to ponder, he did the Grand Tour of France and Italy and left them wondering if their croissants and spaghetti were really here, or in another plane of the universe. Talking of which, some of his theories on space and time would be an early precursor to the way some guy called Einstein would later view the concept. He was also fascinated with nature and, while in Italy, climbed Vesuvius – while it was erupting.

By 1721 George was back in Dublin, becoming a Dean in the Church of Ireland in Derry. The same year Britain was struck by a huge stock market collapse called the South Sea Bubble, during which time companies were selling shares like mad in daft south sea investments such as reclaiming sunshine from rotten vegetables. Countless English eejits bought into it, not unlike the Irish eejits who bought three houses during the Celtic Tiger. Of course the whole thing collapsed and the Westminster Government had to prop up the banking system. Sound familiar? Anyway, Berkeley published a major paper urging a return to a simpler life, the passing of laws restricting consumerism, and the encouragement of the arts. Pretty much what everyone's calling for in Ireland now.

Next George headed for Bermuda where he planned to build an ideal city, including a Christian college to educate the poor savages. But the promised government funding never arrived and he had to abandon his dream. He then returned home to become the Bishop of Cloyne for the remainder of his days, turning his attention to the plight of the poor. He was disgusted by England's treatment of Ireland, economically and socially, and wrote a major paper on the matter called *The Querist*. He lost the run of himself a little towards the end, writing a long treatise on the health benefits of 'tar water', which was a medieval quack cure-all.

He moved briefly to Oxford in 1752 to be with his seriously ill son, who died soon after. George followed him to the grave the following year and was buried in Christ Church, Oxford.

The Berkeley Library in Trinity College honours his memory and, thanks to his American sojourn George also has an entire city named after him – Berkeley, California, home of the world-renowned Berkeley University. How many Irishmen can say that?

ARTHUR GUINNESS

(1724/25–1803)

Probably the most popular man in Irish history, is Arthur. After all, who else has a million glasses raised to him every day of every year? And that's just in the Dáil Bar.

The details of his early days are as cloudy as the head of a pint of his brew, but best guess says he was born near Celbridge around 1724/25, into a middle-class Protestant family. His father worked as land steward for Arthur Price, Archbishop of Cashel, and when the clergyman went to his heavenly reward, he rewarded Arthur with a bequest of £100. He first leased a small brewery in Leixlip when he was 30 and then, deciding he was destined for bigger things, moved to Dublin in 1759 and famously signed a 9000-year lease on a dilapidated brewery at St. James's Gate – clearly he planned to be around for a while.

This might seem like a joke, but at the time drinking beer or stout was much healthier than drinking water as most public supplies would, at best, leave you perched on a jacks for a few days. On top of that, when serious drinking was done, it was usually of the 'hard' variety – people drank illicit poteen that was strong enough to strip paint. So Guinness definitely was 'good for you', or, at least, less bad for

Arthur had a bright idea.

you. As the authorities encouraged beer drinking, Arthur spotted the huge market potential for his distinctive black stout, then called 'porter'. Before long, half the country was getting gee-eyed on his 'healthier alternative', making him a very wealthy man.

In 1761 he married Olivia Whitmore, and one can speculate about the fertility-inducing qualities of the black stuff, as they had, wait for it, 21 children. Poor Olivia must have been permanently knackered. Unfortunately only 10 survived into adulthood, but it was still enough to spawn a dynasty.

By the end of the 1760s, Guinness was being exported and a decade later the brewery began expanding westwards until it was eight times its original size. By 1914 it would be the planet's largest brewery and it's still the world's largest stout brewery. With lots of cash to flash, Arthur proved a generous sort;

It's a little something for the schoolchildren.

he funded schools, and donated to the poor and to hospital funds. He bequeathed his generous nature to successive generations, who gave us, among other things, St. Stephen's Green, the restoration of St. Patrick's Cathedral and lots of social housing.

Fervent nationalists have to swallow a couple of hard facts about Arthur along with their pint, as he was strongly opposed to Irish independence and condemned the 1798 Rebellion. However he also toasted the efforts of Henry Grattan's (P131) Parliament particularly as Grattan wanted to reduce the tax on beer. Arthur was an advocate of Catholic emancipation, probably because 90% of his customers were Catholic.

Arthur is buried in Oughterard, Co. Kildare. A few years ago the town of Celbridge unveiled a statue of him, which gave everybody in the place the excuse to get rat-arsed on his product. Not that any of us ever really need an excuse. Thanks for all the hangovers, Arthur.

OLIVER GOLDSMITH

(1730–1774)

Not many outright dossers earn a place in literary history and a statue in front of Trinity College, but Ollie was that lovable, lazy eejit with talent to burn, and unfortunately, burn much of it he did.

Ever stop fluting around, Goldsmith?

The son of a Protestant clergyman from counties Roscommon, Longford or Westmeath, depending on who shouts the loudest, he went to Trinity where, in theory, he studied law and theology. However the only thing he really learned was to play the flute, cheat at cards and sing Irish ballads while rat-arsed. He was eventually expelled for taking part in a riot. After his father died, relatives paid for him to study medicine in Edinburgh where he soon flunked out, having been unable to find a cure for his own idleness. So Ollie decided to head for Europe, and spent three years doing a walking tour of France, Switzerland and Italy, which was the most energetic thing he'd done all his life, supporting himself by busking with his trusty flute.

He moved to London in 1756, doing odd jobs to support his drinking and gambling, and also tried his hand at writing. At first this was of the hack variety, writing bullshit for pamphlets, or romance or scandal or whatever publishers were prepared to pay for. But at some point he realised he had the ability to do a bit better than this, and began to scribble a few essays, which were published in the well-known journal *The Public Ledger*. Family eyebrows were raised – perhaps there was more to the young gouger after all. When his essays were published in a collection, he found himself considered worthy of the company of famed writers Samuel Johnson and James Boswell. At least now he could get rat-arsed in style.

He continued to gamble, pay for it through hack work, and in between betting, getting drunk and chasing girls, he wrote a respected collection of poetry, followed by a well-received novel called *The Vicar of Wakefield*, a sentimental idealisation of country life, which became one of the most popular novels of the era. He also wrote *The Deserted Village* about the treatment of the rural poor by unscrupulous land-lords. The historian, Horace Walpole, once described him as 'an inspired idiot'. He wasn't wrong; as the money rolled in, it rolled out again just as quickly into gambling dens.

In 1773 Ollie turned his hand to theatre, writing his most famous work *She Stoops to Conquer*, which won rave reviews at the time, and which is still regularly performed. But he barely had time to wallow in his success, as the life of Reilly or rather the death of Reilly finally caught up with him and he died, aged just 44. One can only imagine the heights he might have scaled had it not been for the booze and the debt. And the gambling. And the women.

He was buried in Temple Church in London. There's a monument to him in Ballymahon, Longford, another in Westminster Abbey and of course, the Trinity one, positioned so he can eternally watch all the Dubs heading for the pub but, sadly, never again join them.

HENRY GRATTAN

(1746–1820)

In the 750 years of the Brits poking their noses into Ireland, there were precious few times when we had any respite from their interference. Thanks to Henry Grattan, the end of the eighteenth century gave us a glimmer of light. Well, sort of.

Henry was a Dub, born in Fishamble Street in 1746, where the world-famous Handel's *Messiah* was first performed four years earlier. A Protestant Ascendancy dude, yet he was happy to mix with the lowly Catholic plebs. He studied law in Trinners, and crammed on his oratorical skills, which became so masterful that he could talk a Cavan man out of a penny.

He never really practised law – it wasn't like he needed to earn a living – but in the early 1770s joined The Irish Patriot Party, then headed by Henry Flood, which was campaigning for legislative independence from Britain. But such a gift for the gab had Henry, that he was soon the head honcho, and in 1775, he entered the Irish Parliament, then in College Green. Thanks largely to Grattan, the movement gained lots of support, both from prominent Protestants and especially among Catholics and Presbyterians, which isn't surprising really, as they'd been trodden upon by the Penal Laws for a century. These severely restricted the practice of their religion, property ownership, education, entering political office, and a shedload of other opportunities that were worth having.

After four years in Parliament Henry had per-suaded Westminster to remove many restraints on Irish trade and was pressuring them to repeal the three-centuries-old Poyning's Law, which required us

to ask the British nicely if we could legislate on something and then be grateful if they gave us the nod.

Meantime a large group of armed Protestant men
had formed the Irish Volunteers and Grattan was one
of them. They existed, in theory, to defend Ireland
against a French invasion, but also came in handy
when Grattan started demanding legislative independence. With Grattan constantly nagging Westminster
on the one hand, and this large bunch of armed
guys on the other, the Brits decided in 1782 to save
themselves a lot of hassle and give us Micks a tiny
bit of what we wanted. Henry entered the new-style
Irish Parliament through cheering ranks of Volunteers
and proclaimed: 'I found Ireland on her knees. I have
traced her progress from injuries to arms, and from
arms to liberty. Ireland is now a nation!' Well, not
quite, as most of the population were still fifth-class
citizens, but it was a step in the right direction.

Over the following decade and a half, Grattan
campaigned like a mad yoke to improve the lot of
Catholics and for Catholic Emancipation. But vested
interests, corruption and sneaky Government interference usually left him frustrated. There were too many

people with too much money to lose if, for example, there were changes to Catholic property rights. Henry did manage to get some bits and pieces of legislation through, like allowing Catholics the right to education, to practice law and to practice their religion, but overall his efforts were stymied by wealthy/bigoted gougers in Dublin or London. Grattan repeatedly warned the eejits that their actions were fomenting unrest and that if the British didn't agree to substantial reforms, then bloody rebellion would result. But would they listen? Would they hell.

A vote for Catholics would be the end of civilisation as we know it.

He'd had his fill by 1797, and retired from Parliament, fiercely slagging off the Westminster Government and its lackeys in an open letter to the people of Dublin. Sure enough, the following year, just as he'd predicted, the 1798 Rebellion resulted in over 50,000 deaths, most of them Irish. After that, Westminster decided they'd had enough of this Irish Parliament crap and enacted the Act of Union, meaning that basically we were ruled directly from Britain. Grattan un-retired himself that year in order to campaign against the act, but in vain. His work for independence had linked his name to the rebellion and a lot of ex-buddies now snubbed him and engaged in petty backstabbing, such as removing his portrait from Trinity, striking his name from the Merchant Guild and so on, as if he gave a fiddler's.

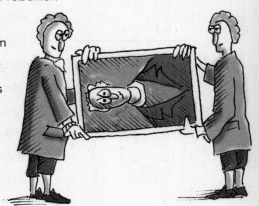

And he did bounce back again, getting elected in 1805 to the British Parliament, and he spent the next 15 years to-ing and fro-ing across the Irish Sea to London to campaign for Catholic Emancipation, alas unsuccessfully. He died in 1820 during one such exhausting jaunt, and the campaign was passed on to Daniel O'Connell (P162).

As the English writer, Sydney Smith, said of Henry: 'He thought only of Ireland; lived for no other object;

dedicated to her his beautiful fancy, his elegant wit, his manly courage, and the splendour of his astonishing eloquence.'

He was buried in Westminster Abbey. There's also a statue in Westminster Palace, and another, in full oratorical flow, outside the old Parliament Building in College Green. Next time you're passing take a sec to give Henry a nod for his very worthy efforts.

JOSEPH HOLT

(1756–1826)

Despite the fact that the 1798 rebellion was banjaxed almost before it began, a handful of its leaders got their tactics bang on when it came to mixing it with the enemy. One such was Joseph Holt.

He was a strange fish. A passionate royalist and Protestant, he was the son of a well-off farmer in Wicklow and took up Daddy's calling by starting his own farm near Roundwood. He was actually employed in several civil offices and even as a sub-constable, and was also a long time member of Henry Grattan's friends, the Irish Volunteers, none of which suggested a future career as a rebel. But he became disillusioned with the parliamentary shenanigans and joined the more radical United Irishmen in 1797, who by then were openly in support of armed revolution.

Next thing Joe knows is that his house is on fire. He, his wife and son survived, but he learned that the blaze was the work of his landlord, who wasn't a fan of the United Irishmen. The arson attack certainly lit a fire under Holtie's arse, as he immediately went off to take part in the 1798 rebellion.

Unfortunately his first real taste of action was at Vinegar Hill, where the rebels were hockeyed. Luckily a large number escaped through a yawning hole in the British ranks. They then fanned out across the country, trying to restart the rebellion, and a large number also made a beeline for the Wicklow Mountains.

Back on home turf, this was when Joseph came into his own. He proved to have superb leadership and organisational skills, and spent the next five months running a guerrilla war, ambushing military targets and then legging it into the hills. In one encounter at Ballyellis, he helped rescue a column of Vinegar Hill survivors who were being pursued

by 200 British soldiers. Joseph ordered a handful of men to stay on the road before a sharp bend, and pretend they were stragglers. Meantime, he positioned his forces behind ditches. The British took the bait, charging in pursuit of the supposed stragglers. Rounding the bend, they realised that the road was blocked by carts and that they were staring at the pike points of hundreds of Irish rebels, who pretty much wiped the poor eejits out.

The campaign continued over the entire summer and Joseph eventually hooked up with another famous rebel, Michael Dwyer (P156). At one point, when short of gunpowder, he reputedly invented an ingenious concoction of God knows what, nicknamed 'Holt's Mixture'. The British, their losses mounting, retreated to a handful of garrisons and hoped Joseph wouldn't turn up and blow them to kingdom come.

But as winter approached and with no sign of the promised large French invasion, the Irishmen were slowly worn down by living in the wilderness. Finally in November, with no hope of victory, Joseph dispersed his men and offered to surrender under terms that he'd be exiled Down Under without trial. Presumably he also fancied some sunshine after wet and windy Wicklow. Keen to get the episode behind them, which had tied down thousands of troops, the British jumped at the chance.

The Holt family arrived in Australia in 1880. In New South Wales Joseph became involved in various intrigues, and was imprisoned a couple of times, accused of plotting Irish insurrections. He farmed for a while, obviously while wearing a daft hat with corks hanging from it, but unbelievably, by 1813, he'd decided he'd had enough glorious sunshine and was pining for the pissing rain back home.

Joseph and the missus attempted to sail back to Ireland on board the *Isabella*, but thanks to a rat-arsed captain, they were shipwrecked on a reef off the Falkland Islands in the South Atlantic. Most of the passengers and crew made it to the tiny Eagle Island; thanks again to Joseph's skills, they survived and were rescued after two months to continue their journey.

In 1814 Joseph settled in what was then Kingstown, but is now Dun Laoghaire, and opened a pub, which was variable in its success giving him ample opportunity to moan about having left Oz. The celestial drinking-up bell sounded for him on May 16th 1826, and his final resting place is in Carrickbrennan Graveyard in Monkstown, surrounded by hundreds of British soldiers who died in a maritime tragedy. A bit ironic, really, as they'd never managed to get that close to him when he was alive.

LORD EDWARD FITZGERALD

(1763–1798)

~

Possibly the most unlikely rebel of all, Lord Eddie was not merely of the wealthier classes but a genuine aristocrat. He was used to fine soirées with princes and nobles, all of whom he would eventually wish to dispatch into the next world.

Born at Carton House in Kildare (now a posh hotel and golf course), his father, the Duke of Leinster, died when he was 10. His mother remarried and moved to the equally humungous Frascati House in Blackrock, Dublin (now demolished), so he wasn't short of playing space. In fact the Fitzgeralds had more houses than a Celtic Tiger property developer, in London, Paris and the south of France. The stepfather, William Ogilvie, filled the spotty youth's head with all sorts of revolutionary stuff, which was a bit rich, considering he was one of the very toffs such revolutions sought to obliterate.

Edward joined the Army at 16. He was packed off to America and fought in the American Revolutionary War, and received a near fatal wound at the Battle of

Eutaw Springs. His life was saved by an escaped slave called Tony Small who found Ed's banjaxed, blood-soaked body, brought him to his cabin and tended his wounds. Lord Edward befriended Tony and hired him as his servant. A few years later, Lord Ed traversed an uncharted region into Quebec on snowshoes, where he made pals of a tribe of Hurons, who adopted him as one of their chiefs.

Back in Europe, Big Chief Edward took off for the revolutionary hotbed of Paris where he heartily toasted 'the speedy abolition of all hereditary titles and feudal distinctions.' While there, the handsome, dashing Eddie fell deeply in love with a young flower called Pamela, who would be no shrinking violet when it later came to supporting his rebellious ideals. They were married in 1792. But while in France, he decided to give up his title, an act that got him thrown out of the army – no great loss to him, since he now regarded them as the enemy.

Returning to Ireland, Edward joined the United Irishmen and began plotting the downfall of the world he'd grown up in. He was soon mixing with Wolfe Tone (P146) and Thomas Russell (P152), and while Tone went off to Paris to muster French support, Russell and he (and Pamela) set off for Hamburg for more secret dealings with the French. It was actually their efforts here that sealed the deal to bring a huge French fleet to Bantry a couple of years later. As they had learned they were under surveillance, it was Pamela who was entrusted to carry the secret papers and plans.

By early 1798, the revolution was almost at hand, and Lord Eddie's charisma and passion had earned him the respect of the rebellion's ordinary foot soldiers. By now he was head of the United Irishmen's military committee and was to be entrusted with leading thousands of men in an attack on New Ross. The English knew he was up to no good, which was all seriously embarrassing for the authorities – an aristocrat mixing it with the riff-raff rebels was just not cricket, by Jove. The Lord Chancellor, Lord Clare, took fright and advised: 'For God's sake, get this young man out of the country; the ports shall be thrown open, and no hindrance offered!'

Just before the rebellion's outbreak, Dublin Castle decided to offer a reward of £1000 for his capture. At the time this would have been enough money to buy about a half a million pints of Guinness, so it was definitely tempting. Lord Edward was forced to go into hiding, but being a bit impulsive, he visited Pamela a couple of times in disguise and also asked his stepfather to visit him, so perhaps it was inevita-

My Lord, there's half a million pints on your head.

ble some scumbag would eventually cop on to his hiding place.

On May 19th, just four days before the rising began, the said scumbag led the authorities to Ed's hiding place in Thomas Street. They burst in brandishing pistols and begged him to surrender peacefully, which would leave the aristocracy less red-faced. But if Eddie was going to miss the rebellion, he was determined to have his own little battle first, so he grappled with the interlopers. He managed to stab a couple of them, one mortally, before he was felled by a shot to the shoulder. Bleeding profusely, he was taken to Newgate Prison, and not being the cleanest spot in the world, his wound became infected, and the dashing Lord Edward died on June 4th. At least he never knew how badly his pet rebellion went.

He was buried in St. Werburgh's Church, Dublin, and ironically, the guy who captured him, Major Henry Sirr, is buried in the churchyard out back. A plaque on the wall honours Edward's memory.

Pamela fled the country because she was up to her neck in subversive stuff and she didn't want the same neck stretched by a rope. In exile in Europe she eventually married some American dude, but she always remained devoted to her dashing aristocratic revolutionary. Her own portrait hangs in the Louvre.

There's a bust of Eddie in Kildare, his home county. But he has perhaps the greatest honour a Dub can confer on one of its heroes – opposite Christ Church Cathedral, near where he was captured, is a pub named after him. And here's a question that might well come up in a pub quiz – name the American Indian chief who was also an Irish rebel? Now you know.

THEOBALD WOLFE TONE

(1763–1798)

He is known as the father of modern Irish republicanism, yet there were doubts about the identity of Theo's own father. Born in Dublin to Peter and Margaret Tone of Kildare, a comfortable Protestant family, Theo was named after his godfather, Margaret's ex-employer, Theobald Wolfe. There was a widespread belief that his Mammy may have dilly-dallied with the boss, Theo being the result.

It seems that he may have inherited some of his mother's libido, as in 1783, while employed as a tutor, he almost had to duel with his employer after having a fling with his missus. But a couple of years later, while studying law at Trinners, he met his future wife Matilda and they eloped. Her parents were royally miffed, but the pair were happily married and would conceive four nippers.

The Tones' Wedding.

Tone soon abandoned law and turned to politics. It was the time of the French Revolution, and Tone and others, Catholic and Protestant, were inspired by the notion of a republic, free from English rule. He thought that Grattan's (P131) pursuit of Catholic Emancipation while remaining loyal to the Crown was as useless as a one-legged man in an arse-kicking contest, and believed that only by uniting all strands of religion in Ireland could one form a true republic. In fact, Theo generally despised all organised religion.

In 1791 he was one of the main founders of the Society of United Irishmen, most of whom were Protestants initially who supported Grattan's efforts to gain freedoms for Catholics. But reform was happening at a snail's pace and the lads became a bit fed up. So around 1794 they decided to abandon that, get lots of guns and blast the feckers out of the country. The British, meantime, weren't too happy to have all this Froggy Revolutionary nuttiness about, so they began to stir the shit between Protestants and Catholics, using the newly formed Orange Order as one of the means of rousing antipathy and violence.

The United Irishmen meantime knew that they probably couldn't win the forthcoming war without help from the French. Unfortunately, as had happened a gansey-load of times before, their plan was betrayed by some bowsie. Half the United Irishmen had to leg it abroad, including Tone, who would spend the next few years in America. Before he went though, he arranged a meeting with a couple of like-minded pals, Thomas Russell and Henry McCracken, on the summit of Cave Hill, overlooking Belfast. They each swore to the 'Cavehill Compact', that was 'Never to desist in our efforts until we subvert the authority of England over our country and assert our independence'.

Theo spent a couple of years in Philly, which he hated, as he thought that the American revolution had simply replaced the British Crown with King Money as the new monarch. He got that one right. So, in 1796, he sailed for France and there used his considerable charisma to persuade Napoleon to supply him with 15,000 men, a fleet of ships and the very distinguished General Hoche at its head. There were also a quarter of a million Irish volunteers ready to do battle for the United Irishmen. We were ready to kick arse.

But talk about bad luck. The entire fleet arrived off Cork during one of the worst storms in a decade and the fleet limped back to France instead of attempting a landing. Had the weather been a teensy weensy bit kinder, our history might be so different – we'd probably have staged the 1916 Rising against our French oppressors instead of the English.

Any chance of more help?

Not tonight, Theobold.

Tone continued his efforts in Paris, but old Boney had other plans for his soldiers and left to kick the crap out of some poor feckers in Egypt. The rising of the following year, 1798, was a disaster. Betrayal led to the arrest of most of the leadership in Dublin, and risings in Antrim, Down, Meath, Kildare and Wicklow were quickly suppressed. The British forces were given carte blanche to commit whatever atrocity took their fancy, and the slaughter was widespread. In Wexford the rebels managed a few victories and kept the rebellion going for several months.

Tone persuaded the French to provide him with more men and ships and, in August, 1000 Frenchies landed at Killala. They enjoyed one of the few decent victories of the rebellion, at Castlebar, but even they were later defeated. The following month Tone arrived at Lough Swilly in Donegal with another 3000 soldiers, only to be intercepted by an English fleet. Tone refused to accept the captain's offer of escape to France and was captured. And with Tone's capture, the rebellion, and the cause of the United Irishmen, fizzled out.

Tone was tried in Dublin, found guilty of treason and sentenced to be hanged. His plea to be shot as a soldier rather than hanged as a traitor was refused. He made a famous speech from the dock:

'From my tenderest youth I have considered the union of Ireland with Great Britain as the scourge of the Irish nation. And that the people of this country can have neither happiness nor freedom whilst that connection endures...and I resolved, if I could, to separate the two countries...to subvert the tyranny of our execrable government and to assert the independence of my country – these were my objects. To unite the whole people of Ireland, and to substitute the common name of Irishman in place of the denominations of Protestant, Catholic and Dissenter – these were my means.'

The following day, Wolfe Tone cut his own throat – but even this was a botch job as it took the poor galoot several days to die.

Wolfe Tone is commemorated annually at his graveside at Bodenstown, County Kildare. A popular Irish band was named after him and there are statues of him all over the place and countless GAA clubs named after him, including many in the USA, Canada, Australia and England. And for the morbidly curious, if you want a gawk at his death mask, it's in St. Michan's Church, Dublin.

THOMAS RUSSELL

(1767–1803)

Thomas Russell was the rebel who missed the rebellion. Twice. Although it must be said that this was through no fault of his own, and he would have charged headlong into battle, given half a chance.

Thomas was born in Cork in 1767 and his father was an officer in the Army. His father was posted to Dublin around 1780 and Thomas joined the Army himself at 16. After three years in India, he returned to Ireland with a growing taste for revolution, and probably one for chicken curry as well.

But one thing he didn't have was a sweet tooth: from his early days, Thomas fervently campaigned against slavery, and sugar was slave-produced in the West Indies. As he put it himself: 'on every lump of sugar I see a drop of human blood'. No sherbet suckers for him.

He spent a few years studying politics and science, and was visiting the Irish Parliament in 1790 when he bumped into Wolfe Tone. The pair were soon enthusing about all the aristocratic heads being removed in Paris. That meeting charted the course of his life – which unfortunately wouldn't be all that long.

A couple of years later in Belfast he began mingling with others of like mind and helped to convince many prominent Presbyterians that they should embrace their Catholic neighbours, metaphorically speaking, if they wanted real change. Within a year he'd completely burned his British bridges as he and Tone were among those who met in Belfast on 1791 to form the United Irishmen, whose radical ideas didn't exactly make them buddies of the Crown.

When England and France decided to start batin' the bejaysus out of each other in 1793, the United Irishmen, given their fondness for revolution French-style, were suddenly viewed with suspicious eyes, and the next thing guys with big guns were battering down their doors. Russell and friends secretly continued their activities, spreading the word throughout Ireland with pamphlets, covert meetings and rousing ballads that people sang while getting fluthered. Those declaring loyalty to the United Irishmen swelled to over a quarter of a million.

In 1796, Russell published a pamphlet entitled *A Letter to the People of Ireland*, suggesting that the revolution was at hand and how the United Irishmen would transform Ireland economically and socially, and that really got up the authorities' noses. So the soldiers came knocking at his door, or to be precise, kicking it in, and hauled him off to a prison in the Scottish Highlands for six years. As a result, he missed the 1798 rebellion, which might have been a stroke of luck in hind-

The view from Russell's Highland cell.

sight. But having missed out on one rebellion, he was determined to have a crack at the next one.

On his release in 1802, Russell headed straight for France in search of tips on revolution. There he met Robert Emmet, and learned of his plans for another rebellion. Unfortunately old Boney wouldn't give 'les pesky Irlandais' any more soldiers. Not to be put off, Russell sneaked back in disguise to Ireland to recruit new members in the north for the upcoming mayhem.

And mayhem it was, because if the 1798 Rising went badly, the 1803 Rising went completely arseways. Russell spent weeks literally galloping around the north trying to encourage people to take up arms, but the memory of 1798 was still fresh, and nobody was too keen to have their insides turned into out-sides. The insurrection went ahead in Dublin on July 23rd, with a completely knackered Thomas Russell stuck in the north, so the rebellion, in effect, passed him by. Again.

In the aftermath, he rather naively decided to flee to Dublin (the centre of the action) to hide, and he was tracked down a few months later. He was taken back north to Downpatrick Gaol, and hanged there for treason on October 21st.

You couldn't fault Thomas Russell for his valiant efforts, but sadly, as regards Ireland's freedom, it was yet another dead end. Literally.

MICHAEL DWYER

(1772–1825)

In our various conflicts with the English down the centuries, one of the few areas where we excelled was at guerrilla warfare. It was certainly a no-brainer for Michael Dwyer, who like Joseph Holt (P136), conducted a guerrilla war against the English in the Wicklow mountains, but unlike Holt, held out for an amazing five years.

Born to Catholic tenant farmer parents in Wicklow's Glen of Imaal, Michael's education was in a hedge school, and it was here he learned of the American and French Revolutions, so he was rarin' to take part in Ireland's glorious revolution by the time he was shaving.

He joined the United Irishmen in 1797 and a year later he served as a captain in the wojus disasters of Vinegar Hill and the Battle of Arklow. He was under Holt's command when he got his first taste of guerrilla warfare – and victory – at Ballyellis (P137). Clearly this strategy was the way to go.

Michael used the hills and forests to great effect, attacking small outposts, then getting the hell out, and vanishing into the mountains. Holt surrendered as 1798 drew to a close, but Dwyer wasn't done by a long shot. He was a natural leader and organiser and won the admiration of his men with his personal courage. Split into small, fast-moving groups, the rebels raided the farms of local loyalists for supplies, attacked countless small bands of soldiers and slowly forced the British to retreat to their strongholds. This became a serious pain for them as thousands of troops were locked up in barracks, scratching their arses waiting for some rebels to massacre. Eventually they were forced to build a long road (the Military Road, which still exists) into the mountains so they could move quickly into Dwyer's territory.

It'll be handy to hunt down Dwyer's rebels... and hillwalkers.

SALLY GAP

One of the most heroic episodes of his five-year campaign happened in February 1799, at a place called Doire na Muc (anglicised Dernamuck) in west Wicklow. Several groups of Michael's forces were in hiding among civilians in cottages scattered about the area. Unfortunately some sleeveen sold them out, and that night hundreds of English soldiers surrounded the cottages. With the situation hopeless, two groups surrendered – and were subsequently hanged for their trouble. Michael Dwyer occupied the third cottage with three others – Sam McAllister, John Savage and Patrick Costello – and they commenced a fight to the death against a gazillion soldiers. Very soon the cottage looked like a colander, and Costello and Savage lay dead. McAllister was badly wounded and in an act of incredible bravery, and against Dwyer's wishes, told his leader to make his escape while he drew the enemy fire. He pulled open the door and was felled by a rain of bullets, and while they reloaded, Michael fled into the night. He was pursued for hours but eventually escaped by swimming a river and disappearing into the hills. The cottage was purchased by the state in the 1940s and you can still visit it.

He continued his guerrilla campaign all the way to 1803 – in effect from one rebellion to the next. He actually met with Emmet (P169) but wasn't convinced of his chances of success – he clearly had his head screwed on. He told Emmet he would only commit his forces if the uprising in Dublin showed early promise. When it failed miserably, he once again returned to the wilds.

After a second rebellion in five years, the authorities were really getting miffed and decided to put an end to all this uprising business. Michael was one of their principal targets. They couldn't root him out so the gougers started a campaign of violent intimidation against suspected sympathisers. Desperate to put an end to the suffering of innocent civilians, Michael eventually offered to surrender in December 1803 on condition he and his family be exiled to the USA. The authorities agreed, accepted his surrender and then the bastards reneged on the deal, as was their custom. He and his family were first imprisoned for high treason in Kilmainham Gaol, but ultimately spared execution and exiled to Australia. He would never see his beloved Wicklow again.

He lived for another 19 years Down Under, became a successful farmer, was involved in various intrigues with the local British bigwigs and accused of plotting rebellion. He survived all of that and was even appointed Chief of Police in Liverpool, New South Wales, but sadly that ended when he got fluthered one night and lost a pile of important documents. His farm business went downhill and by 1825 he hadn't two pennies to rub together. Briefly thrown into the debtor's prison, it proved to be a death sentence as he contacted dysentery there and died in August 1825.

There is a statue of Michael in the Glen of Imaal in Wicklow and one of Sam McAllister in Baltinglass, County Wicklow. As he left seven children in Oz, there are now gazillions of O'Dwyers there, and they all get together every once in a while to down a few scoops in memory of the man they know as 'The Wicklow Chief'.

Howya, howya, howya?

DANIEL O'CONNELL

(1775–1847)

You might have heard of this guy. He's the one with the big street named after him. Where? Oh, the one in Dublin, Ennis, Sligo, Clonmel, Athlone, Kilkee, Waterford, Melbourne, New York, Sydney, Arkansas, Liverpool etc. Dan the Man was obviously something special, and after centuries of unrest, it was he who finally gave us a bit of peace and quiet.

Dan was born near Cahirciveen in Kerry and raised by a wealthy uncle, but he mixed happily with the locals and liked an oul' tune on the fiddle. At 16 he said farewell to the scenery and lousy weather, and continued his education in France, also learning a thing or two about how French revolutionaries liked to chop people's heads off.

Dan returned to Ireland a few years later and realised that, although he was extremely brainy, he'd be denied entry to the élite ranks because he was a Catholic, while complete gobshites were getting all the good jobs. It began to dawn that British policy was effectively to maintain the wealth and power of the Protestant Ascendancy. Something would have to be done.

Dan qualified as a barrister in May 1798, and a few days later the country exploded in mayhem. While he agreed with French revolutionary aims, he felt beheading, hanging, burning and disembowelling was not the way to proceed.

He started a legal practice in Munster and became very wealthy, although because of his taste for the good life, he spent money almost as quickly as he earned it, and was in debt for much of his life. In 1802 he fell in love with his cousin, Mary O'Connell, and they would enjoy a long, happy marriage, which produced four sons and three daughters.

After the 1803 rebellion, he defended rebels in court because he knew what had motivated them – and that there was gallons of blood on the hands of those men's accusers. But he was really getting tired of all the chaos and said of Emmet (P169): 'A man who could coolly prepare so much bloodshed and such horrors has ceased to be an object of compassion'. Clearly not a fan. There had to be another way.

In 1811 he founded the Catholic Board, which took
the first baby steps along the road to his principal
aim, Catholic Emancipation. In the next few years he
openly slagged the authorities, calling the privileged
shower of savages all sorts of names and demanding
an end to their monopoly of the positions of power.
Dan was becoming a serious pain in the arse to
the establishment. When, in 1815, he called Dublin
Corpo 'that beggarly corporation', one of them, a
renowned duellist called D'Esterre, threw down the
gauntlet and challenged him. The boys in Dublin
Castle were rubbing their hands at the prospect of
seeing a large bullet hole in O'Connell. But despite
his horror of violence, Dan turned out to be a better
shot than D'Esterre, and hit him in the hip, from which
injury he later died. Dan's conscience was so both-

ered afterwards that he completely renounced all violence and paid part of his income to support D'Esterre's family for the rest of his days.

In 1823, he set up the Catholic Association, which openly supported such stuff as electoral reform, tenants' right and repeal of anti-Catholic laws. Membership cost just one penny a month, so even the poorest Catholics could join up – and they did in vast numbers. The money raised supported emancipation candidates, and very slowly, official opinion began to swing towards Dan's aims.

Then in 1828 he took the bull by the horns and stood for election to the House of Commons – a Catholic hadn't seen the inside of the gaff for over a century. Dan enjoyed a landslide victory in Ennis, but couldn't take his seat because he'd have to take the Oath of Supremacy, which for a Catholic, was like a turkey swearing allegiance to Christmas.

165

The Brits now had a serious problem – if he wasn't allowed to take his seat at Westminster, they'd probably have another damn uprising on their hands. Faced with six or seven million screaming Irish folk, they withered and finally passed the Emancipation Act, which removed many of the shackles that had suppressed Catholics, and admitted Catholics and Presbyterians to Parliament. It was a huge victory for O'Connell and earned him the nickname of 'The Liberator'. He finally took his seat in July 1829.

He now turned his rather brainy head towards the Repeal of the Act of Union – he wanted Ireland to rule herself, although he was prepared to allow Britain's monarch to remain head of state. This would be a much tougher nut to crack.

What didn't help his cause was the Tithe War in the 1830s. This was an outbreak of serious violence by Catholic tenant farmers who didn't like the idea of paying tithes (a tenth of their income) to the local Protestant clergyman. There were hundreds of deaths on both sides. Dan successfully defended many of those accused of the violence.

Meantime he was busy working on the Repeal of the Union, and he had an idea how to get things moving – a very large idea. He started to organise 'monster meetings', and literally hundreds of thousands of people attended meetings in Cork, Tipp, Wexford and Limerick. O'Connell was a brilliant orator and the crowd's cheers were so loud they could be heard miles away. These had the authorities crapping in their pants, especially when O'Connell organised a meeting at the symbolic hill of Tara – seat of the ancient high kings – that was attended by half a million people.

The British eventually came up with the answer to O'Connell's passive resistance strategy – blow as many innocent people to bits as they could. Meantime O'Connell planned to make his next meeting the biggest and most symbolic yet. It would take place at Clontarf – the scene of Brian Boru's victory. The British sent two warships into Dublin carrying 3000 troops and threatened that if the meeting went ahead, the soldiers would train their guns on the (unarmed) crowd. Really brave of them. Dan could not contemplate the possibility of a massacre in his name – he was a pacifist after all – and so he called off the meeting at the last moment. Then the Brits had him arrested, charged with conspiracy and jailed for a year, although the conviction was later quashed and he was released after three months.

Now heading for his seventies, his health was failing. A couple of years later the Famine struck and all thoughts of Repeal were pushed aside. He spent his last years campaigning for help for Famine victims and, in his final speech in the House of Commons, he predicted that if the British didn't send help 'one quarter of [Ireland's] population will perish'. The help didn't come and Dan's figure was amazingly accurate.

He left Ireland for warmer climes on doctor's advice in 1847, bound for Rome. He stopped in Paris and was greeted by huge crowds of cheering Frenchmen who called him 'the most successful champion of liberty and democracy in Europe'. Sadly Dan never reached the Eternal City, but died in Genoa on May 15th. According to his wishes, his heart was buried in Rome and his body returned to Glasnevin Cemetery, where it lies under probably the largest tomb monument in Ireland – a massive round tower.

Dan the Man's fame spread far and wide and he inspired leaders all over the world, such as Gandhi and Martin Luther King. Even Britain's PM Gladstone conceded that O'Connell was 'the greatest popular leader the world has ever seen', and famous writers, politicians and philosophers lined up to shower him with compliments. He wasn't quite so popular in America's southern states, however, for his condemnation of slavery and his friendship with Frederick Douglass – a former slave who became a leader of the abolitionist movement. But who cared what they thought?

There are so many monuments to Dan it is impossible to list them, so let's sign off with a famous quote of his: 'The altar of liberty totters when it is cemented only with blood.' You said it, Dan.

ROBERT EMMET

(1778–1803)

Amazing the power of words, as were it not for Emmet's speech from the dock after his trial for treason, he would probably just have played a bit part in Irish history. Instead, he's one of the most recognisable names from our past, and there's no denying his vision, courage or idealism. He just didn't have any bleedin' luck.

His was the rebellion that never was, or at least that only half was, if even that. He was born into a posh Protestant family who lived in St. Stephen's Green, Dublin. His parents were sympathetic to downtrodden Catholics and were also fans of the American Revolution.

Robert's big brother Thomas was a member of the United Irishmen and a pal of Wolfe Tone, and Tone regularly popped into the Emmet household for tea and scones and a bit of subversive natter, so Robert's education as a rebel began when he was just waist high. At 15 he started his studies at

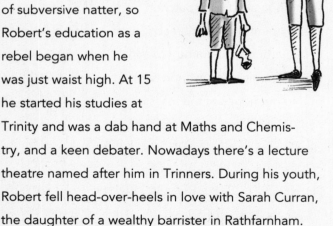

Trinity and was a dab hand at Maths and Chemistry, and a keen debater. Nowadays there's a lecture theatre named after him in Trinners. During his youth, Robert fell head-over-heels in love with Sarah Curran, the daughter of a wealthy barrister in Rathfarnham. The old man didn't approve of Emmet however, and would later disown his daughter for becoming engaged to Robert. Tragically, his love of Sarah would ultimately prove his undoing.

After the 1798 rebellion, Robert became involved in re-organising the tattered remnants of the United Irishmen, which brought the attentions of the authorities, and he had to leg it abroad as a wanted man. He spent the next couple of years in France trying to organise more French help, but it never materialised, so he decided that we'd just have to boot out the Brits by ourselves.

He returned to Ireland in 1802 and began to make plans for the following year. He dispatched co-conspirators like Thomas Russell (P152) around the country to stir up support, which was in short supply, due to memories of the massacres of 1798. He started manufacturing weapons in people's gaffs all around Dublin. He used his knowledge of chemistry to make gunpowder and even invented a pike that folded in half, so you could hide it under

Early prototype of the "Emmet Easy-Fold" pike.

a cloak, then whip it out and gut some poor fecker before he knew jack shit about it.

Unfortunately, all this secrecy and planning was undermined when some gobshite dropped a cigar or something on gunpowder in one of the safe houses, and when you do that... well, we've all seen the cartoons. After this mysterious explosion, the authorities started scratching their heads and asking, 'Now why would anyone have a big pile of gunpowder stored in their living room?'

So Robert was forced to move his insurrection forward, which was a really bad idea, as he'd barely recruited enough rebels to make a hurling team. But the show had to go on, and so on July 23rd 1803, Emmet led the tiny band of rebels against Dublin Castle. Not surprisingly, that plan didn't work out too well, and they retreated to Thomas Street, where they kinda turned into a raving mob. They pulled a lone dragoon from his horse and piked the virtually defenceless fecker to death. They then chanced upon the Lord Chief Justice, Lord Kilwarden, and his nephew in a carriage. These were also dragged out and butchered. This wasn't exactly part of Emmet's vision and when he failed to stop the murderous rampaging, he decided he'd had enough and abandoned the insurrection. After a night of hacking and shooting, 50 rebels and 20 soldiers lay dead, as did the 1803 rebellion.

Emmet hid in the Wicklow Mountains for a while, but couldn't bear to be away from Sarah Curran, and sneaked back into Dublin to see her in a small house beside Harold's Cross Bridge (nowadays Emmet Bridge). The authorities got wind this and descended on the place on August 25th, hauling Emmet off to Kilmainham Gaol. From there he wrote love letters to Sarah, which certainly did no harm his image as a dashing, courageous, romantic figure.

He was tried for treason on September 19th and sentenced to be executed. His final speech from the dock assured his immortality:

Let no man write my epitaph; for as no man who knows my motives dare now vindicate them, let not prejudice or ignorance, asperse them. Let them and me rest in obscurity and peace, and my tomb remain uninscribed, and my memory in oblivion. When my country takes her place among the nations of the earth, let my epitaph be written. I have done.

He was hanged and beheaded the following day in Thomas Street, although because he was of an aristocratic background, he was not disembowelled. Very considerate. There are various theories as to what happened to his body, but his burial place remains a mystery and his epitaph remains unwritten.

There's a statue of Robert Emmet in St. Stephen's Green and one in Washington DC, another in San Francisco. Places named after him in the USA include counties in Iowa and Michigan, and towns in Nebraska and Iowa. He's also the subject of a song by Thomas Moore and a poem by Shelley, and the great American writer, Washington Irving, dedicated a book to Robert and Sarah's love for each other. It seems that dying young and in love has made him immortal.

ANNE DEVLIN

(1780–1851)

Women are conspicuous by their near-absence from Irish history's hall of fame. It wasn't that women didn't play their part, but due to the hierarchy of the day, they were kept in the background, and rarely given credit for their actions. But Anne certainly earned her fame – her bravery makes most fellas look like wimps.

She was born in Rathdrum, Wicklow, and the fact that she was a niece of Michael Dwyer (P156) and that her father was imprisoned for rebellious activities pretty much charted her future leanings. The family moved to Rathfarnham in Dublin after the 1798 rebellion because they were fed up with the authorities kicking their door down. Robert Emmet (P169) also had a house nearby and it was a hive of subversive activity, which he feared might attract attention.

So he hired Anne as his housekeeper, her duties involving the normal household management stuff – cooking, laundry, hiding gunpowder under the floor-boards, concealing guns in the airing cupboards and carrying secret messages.

Soon after the disastrous insurrection in 1803, Emmet's house was raided and Anne was seized by the local yeomanry. They tortured her by half-hanging her and prodding her with bayonets in an attempt to extract information about Emmet, who was on the run. She didn't reveal a word; the gougers assumed she knew nothing and released her.

She returned to her family home, but her trouble was only starting as another senior gouger in Dublin Castle, Major Henry Sirr (the guy who arrested Lord Edward Fitzgerald, P141), had the entire Devlin family, children and all, arrested and thrown into Kilmainham. Anne was put into a squalid cell. She was again tortured, and again refused to talk. After Emmet was captured, he urged Anne to inform on his activities as he was already doomed, but she still refused for fear of incriminating others. Weeks of torture having failed, the bastards then tried bribery – offering her £500 if she would give up conspirators' names, a sum that would have kept her family in comfort for decades. She basically told them where to stick their wad of notes. They finally realised they couldn't break her, but out of spite, continued to keep her and her family in prison until her nine-year-old brother died of malnutrition and dysentery brought about by the conditions.

After this, her family was released but Anne lingered in prison until 1806. On her release she tried to pick up the tattered threads of her life. She married a drayman called William Campbell and moved into the Liberties. As an old woman her life descended into extreme poverty and, eventually, starvation. Anne died alone in a slum called Little Elbow Lane. Before she died, a Carmelite monk called Luke Cullen recorded her story and, were it not for his efforts, her memory would probably have been wiped from history. Her courage and loyalty were finally recognised when a statue of her was unveiled in Rathfarnham, almost two centuries after the insurrection.

FR. THEOBALD MATHEW

(1790–1856)

Let's leave politics for the moment and turn to drink. Or rather, turn away from drink. Because that's what Fr. Mathew persuaded us to do in our millions.

He was born in Tipp to parents of Welsh stock and had a private education in Thurles and Kilkenny. By the time he was 17 he'd had a calling from God, and God directed him to Maynooth, where he joined the Capuchin Order. He was ordained in Dublin in 1813 and after a year transferred to Cork.

There's a legend that he was a heavy drinker in his younger days and one night had a vision of a strange bird, which he saw as a sign to change his ways. Now while many rat-arsed men have visions involving strange birds, usually they just forget about it the next day due being nearly dead with the hangover Not Fr. Matthew, who took it upon himself to change the drinking habits of the nation. (Anyway, the story is probably apocryphal as the Capuchin Order is devoted to austerity and poverty, so it's unlikely they were passing around the booze every night.)

'Who's a pissed boy then?'

Many Irish people enjoy a drink or 10, in case you hadn't heard. It was no different back then, except that it wasn't designer lagers and the like – no, we were addicted to the hard stuff, poteen, and basically the country was drowning in it. Fr. Mathew decided it was time to call last orders and founded the Cork Total Abstinence Society in 1838. He then began travelling the country preaching the evils of alcohol and asking people to take 'The Pledge' i.e. never to let a drop of the devil's brew pass their lips again. Considering all the ineffective anti-alcohol ad campaigns that governments waste money on nowadays,

Fr. Mathew must have been some communicator, because he persuaded a massive four million to take the pledge – half the population of the day! Dan O'Connell (P162) said his movement brought about a 'great moral change', and the stats are impressive. In the first three years of his campaign, the number of people sent to prison fell by a third. Homicides were reduced by two-thirds, robberies by three-quarters and death sentences fell by 80%.

In 1842 he went international and is reputed to have gotten over a million people to go on the dry in England. It was then off to the Big

Business has gone through the floor

Apple in 1849, where he was greeted like a miracu-lous saviour by the Mayor, and New Yorkers queued for days to reject the demon drink. President Zach-ary Taylor even invited him to dinner in the White House, where presumably only water was served. And Congress and the Senate bestowed their highest honours on him. He then toured 20 states and persuaded over half a million formerly fluthered Yanks to climb on the wagon. The only blot on Fr. Matthew's copybook came in the southern states – they demanded his anti-alcohol lectures should not also be anti-slavery lectures. Conflicted, he avoided condemning slavery in his speeches, and was himself condemned by abolitionists.

He returned to Ireland in 1851 but his health began to fail, and the shutters were finally pulled down on him in 1856. He was buried in St. Joseph's Cemetery in Cork.

There are statues of Fr. Mathew in Cork, Dublin, Limerick, and in Salem, Massachusetts. It was estimated that he'd persuaded seven million people to take the pledge. None of the statues were sponsored by breweries or distilleries.

JAMES CLARENCE MANGAN

(1803–1849)

Turning our thoughts to matters literary, we now meet one of Ireland's finest poets. James Mangan (the 'Clarence' bit was added in his teens, probably as a pretentious adolescent rebellious thing) was born in Dublin. His father was a bit of a loser, failed in several business ventures and liked the odd tipple, so poor James had a tough start. At 15, he was forced

Mangan scrivening

to get a job as a 'scrivener', or clerk, which he found as boring as a Fianna Fáil Ard Fheis, so it must have been sheer torture.

Meantime he was scribbling away by candlelight, and he eventually began submitting verses to various publications, and having them printed to generous reviews. He wasn't short of the oul' grey matter, either, and managed to learn German, Latin, Spanish, French, Italian and even Irish (tougher than all the others put together.) By his early thirties he was translating the German masterpieces of Goethe, and also literary stuff from Turkish, Persian and Arabic. He was a handy sort with the lingos. And yet acclaim for his poetry eluded him, and he slowly drifted into booze and opium addiction. He also went a bit wonky in the noggin and would wander the streets dressed in a blond wig, a conical hat, trousers four times too large and green glasses.

But when the Great Famine struck James found inspiration, and produced a gansey-load of great poetry with a political slant. His poems such as 'Róisín Dubh', 'A Vision of Connaught in the Thirteenth Century' and 'Siberia' portrayed the Ireland of his time through another time or place. This bit from 'Siberia' gives a glimpse of how he saw hunger-ravaged Ireland:

> In Siberia's wastes
> Are sands and rocks.
> Nothing blooms of green and soft
> But the snowpeaks rise aloft
> And the gaunt ice-blocks.

His work caught the eye of the lads in *The Nation* (P188) and he was soon rubbing shoulders with rebels, who chose to ignore his conical hat because his poetry was so good. Unfortunately being pals with the rebels proved disastrous for James; after the failed Rising of 1848, he was dismissed from his job in Trinity and spiralled into decline.

By June of 1849 he'd hit rock bottom and was discovered by William Wilde, Oscar's Da, living in 'a state of indescribable misery, occupying a wretched hovel where he had retired to die'. And sadly, die he did, soon after, in the Meath Hospital. He was buried in Glasnevin and his contemporary headstone describes him as 'Ireland's National Poet'. You can also see a bust of James in the middle of St. Stephen's Green.

He was described by WB Yeats as one of the greatest Irish poets. He said: 'To the soul of Clarence Mangan was tied the burning ribbon of Genius.' So the last word goes to this gifted, colourful character:

I could scale the blue air
I could plough the high hills
O, I could kneel all night in prayer
To heal your many ills!
And one beamy smile from you
Would float like light between
My toils and me, my own, my true
My Dark Rosaleen!
My fond Rosaleen!
Would give me life and soul anew
A second life, a soul anew
My Dark Rosaleen!

THE YOUNG
IRELANDERS:

John Blake Dillon (1814–1866)
Thomas Davis (1814–1845)
Charles Gavan Duffy (1816–1903)
William Smith O'Brien (1803–1864)
John Mitchel (1815–1875)
Thomas Francis Meagher (1823–1867)
James Fintan Lalor (1807–1849)

A whole bunch of famous Irishmen sprang from the Young Irelanders' movement and much of their lives and fates were intertwined. So to save the hassle of interminably repeating the events of the mid-1840s, and boring you to tears, here's the whole shebang.

After Daniel O'Connell (P162) backed away from an armed conflict at Clontarf, some of O'Connell's Repeal Association started to have their own ideas about how to get results. They were John Blake

Dillon, Thomas Osborne Davis and Charles Gavan Duffy.

John Blake Dillon was born in Roscommon to middle-class parents, and was off to Trinity as a youth to study law. While there he became friends with another student, **Thomas Davis**, a Corkonian whose father was a doc in the British Army. He too was studying for the Bar, and soon Davis and Dillon realised they shared similar rebellious notions. After college they both got jobs working for *The Morning Register*, a Catholic newspaper, and there they came to the attention of the last of the initial Young Ireland trio, **Charles Gavan Duffy**. Unlike the others, Duffy came from (relatively) humble beginnings. The son of a Dublin shopkeeper, he studied at a posh Catholic school in Belfast. He too became a law student but he was also a decent hand at penning the odd verse or two.

All three were members of O'Connell's Repeal Association, and as they still had some lingering pubescent acne, they were given the nickname The Young Irelanders. Their relative youth also made them impatient and, despite O'Connell's earlier successes, they became fed up with monster meetings not producing results quick enough. There had to be a faster way – like firing guns at the enemy.

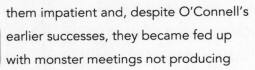

Not exactly what I had in mind.

They decided to go out on their own, not as militant rebels, but as newspapermen, and launched *The Nation*, a republican publication. Unlike most newspapers at the time, which recorded Britain's glorious victories and how they brought civilisation to ignorant mucksavages like us Irish, *The Nation* offered a slightly different perspective: namely, the British were oppressive gougers who should feck off and leave us alone. *The Nation* and The Young Irelanders soon attracted lots of other chaps who would make a name for themselves. Among these were William Smith O'Brien, John Mitchel, Thomas Francis Meagher and James Fintan Lalor.

William Smith O'Brien was a posh Clareman whose gaff was none other than Dromoland Castle, now a five-star hotel catering for the likes of Bill Clinton and Nelson Mandela (and even Bertie Ahern, but hey, let's not hold that against them). William was a Protestant who supported Catholic Emancipation from an early age, and he wasn't so much a Young Irelander as a Middle Aged Irelander, because while the others were nearly still in short pants, he was the MP for Ennis.

Thomas Francis Meagher was a brainy, middle-class Catholic from Waterford, who excelled at public speaking. He joined the Repeal Association but believed that, if the pacifist thing didn't work out, it would be quite honourable to blow the feckers to hell. Obviously the pragmatic type. But probably his most famous contribution to Irish history was the thing you wave above your head on Paddy's Day. No, not the inflatable leprechaun – the Irish Tricolour.

John Mitchel was one interesting head-the-ball: he has a reputation as a great patriot, but sadly was also a bleedin' racist, especially in later life. He was born to a Protestant family in Derry and was a child prodigy, apparently learning the rudiments of Latin, aged five, and reading ancient classical works, aged seven. He got his degree in Trinity and, like half of middle-class Ireland, became a lawyer. Despite being a Proddie, he hated the sight of Orangemen deliberately detouring through Catholic areas during historical commemorations (some things never change). They would stop provocatively to play a few tunes and chant Orange slogans, which, not surprisingly, often resulted in heads being battered on both sides. Mitchel was known for defending Catholics in court after these incidents.

James Fintan Lalor was born to middle-class Catholics in Laois. His father, Patrick, was the first Catholic MP for Laois and campaigned fiercely against tithes. When Patrick's sheep were to be taken in lieu of unpaid tithes, he cleverly painted 'Tithe' on each of them, so that no other Irish farmer would buy them. James would turn out to be even more radical than his Da, and was probably the most militant of all the Young Irelanders – something which got him expelled from O'Connell's Repeal Association. He also suffered from a painful spinal disease, which affected his posture – but he never let a weensy thing like being a cripple get in the way of fighting for Ireland. He believed repeal of the union was a side issue and that the real meat in the sandwich of Irish oppression were the downtrodden tenant farmers – in that respect he was ahead of his time, as Davitt and Parnell would make this their focus decades later. He also had a knack with the writing, a skill that would attract the guys' attention at *The Nation*, who were always on the lookout for a decent fanatical anti-British scribe. The call wouldn't be long coming.

But back to the original Young Irelanders. By 1845, Thomas Davis had established himself as a noted republican writer and poet. You may have heard the little ditty 'A Nation Once Again', which gives a hint of his leanings. His poems, essays and articles would later become a gospel for rebels like Pádraig Pearse. At this point *The Nation* had a quarter of a million readers and the Young Irelanders' vision was gathering momentum. But sadly, Thomas Davis wouldn't get to play any further part, because he contacted scarlet fever and died, aged just 30. He is immortalised with a statue in College Green, Dublin, unveiled by Dev in 1966. It would have pleased him no end that his statue took a spot long occupied by King Billy.

Gavan Duffy and Blake Dillon invited John Mitchel to take over from Davis and, as the Famine took hold, he wrote brilliant, graphic articles about its effects and openly vilified Britain. He would later leave *The Nation* because he thought it was a bit soft on the British. He formed his own newspaper, *The United Irishman*, which was anything but – its first editorial was an open letter addressed to 'Her Majesty's Executioner-General and Butcher of Ireland' aka the Lord Lieutenant, Lord Clarendon. The newspaper was shut down after just 16 editions, surprise, surprise. Mitchel was arrested, tried for treason felony, which is like 'treason lite', and sentenced to transportation to Van Diemen's Land (Tasmania) for 14 years. That was two Young Irelanders down, and not a shot fired.

One of Mitchel's chief supporters had been James Fintan Lalor, who contributed a whole series of articles slagging the hell out of Britain's landlord class, who were, he claimed, 'forcing self-defence on us.' His writings would later influence land reformer Michael Davitt and 1916 rebels Pearse and Connolly, and his rallying cry became 'the land of Ireland for the people of Ireland', a slogan that endured for generations. Like Mitchel, he eventually left *The Nation* to set up a more radical paper called *The Irish Felon*, taking its name from the British habit of labelling Irish nationalists 'felons'. The content didn't mince its words:

'...somewhere and somehow, and by somebody, a beginning must be made. Who strikes the first blow for Ireland? Who draws first blood?'

The Irish Felon only survived a few months, as unfortunately so would its proprietor.

Charles Gavan Duffy was the editor of *The Nation*, and as the Famine worsened, he used the paper to suggest that it was time to dust off the old muskets in the attic as the British clearly didn't give a fiddler's fart about the starving. Next thing he and the others knew, they were being dragged off to the slammer. *The Nation* was closed down and Duffy tried for sedition. His defence counsel was another leading light of Irish history, Isaac Butt. Try as they might, the British couldn't get a damn conviction, so they just kept trying him again and again – there were four trials in all – until eventually they threw in the towel and released him.

Meantime, also in 1848, Meagher and O'Brien went to France to do a course in how to achieve maximum enemy bloodshed with minimum effort, the French having had recent experience. And it was here that Thomas Meagher acquired the Tricolour, when he was given it by some French ladies sympathetic to Ireland's plight. Meagher unveiled the new green, white and orange flag in Waterford – green for nationalists, orange for Orangemen and white for the peace between them (dream on), but it actually wouldn't come into widespread use until it was unfurled on the top of the GPO during the 1916 Rising.

It was a hectic year, 1848, what with raids, trials, new flags and so on, and things were also hotting up on the rebellion front.

Because the Famine was in full swing, the Young Irelanders mistakenly believed that the rage provoked by starvation would rouse people to insurrection, but in fact most had only one thing on their minds – eating. Actually, John Blake Dillon wasn't that keen on taking up arms, but went along as that's what Meagher, O'Brien, Dillon et al wanted. The Young Irelanders travelled through Wexford, Kilkenny and Tipperary trying to stir the people to action. Finally, at Ballingarry in Tipp, they roused enough anti-British feeling to attract the attention of the local constabulary. A stand-off ensued with the police hiding in a cottage holding children as hostages, and in the ensuing gunfight two locals were killed. When constabulary reinforcements arrived the rebels disappeared into the night, as did the pimple-sized rebellion of 1848. In fact, for all their collective intelligence, this was probably the worst-planned, worst-equipped and worst-executed uprising in Irish history.

John Blake Dillon fled to the USA disguised as a priest. He got a job there as a lawyer and after an amnesty in Ireland in 1855, he returned and entered politics. His stint as a rebel had warmed him to Tipperary hearts, so they duly elected him as an MP in 1865. He had by now renounced violence and was campaigning for a federal union between Britain and Ireland, but we'll never know how that might have turned out, as he died of cholera from infected water, aged 52.

John Fintan Lalor was arrested, tried for treason felony and thrown into Nenagh Gaol, but was so sick they released him the following month. Amazingly, despite his ill-health and the failure of the July Rising, he tried to stage another 'rebellion' in September, attacking an RIC barracks in Cappoquin in Waterford. This also failed miserably to rouse the country to action, as half the population was either dead or half-way there. He was again arrested, but died in prison of bronchitis, aged just 42. His funeral was a massive affair attended by 25,000. In 2007 a statue of him was unveiled in Portlaois.

William Smith O'Brien was captured, found guilty of treason, and sentenced to be hanged, drawn and quartered. A petition signed by 100,000 Irish folk demanding clemency made the Brits rub their chin thoughtfully and his sentence was commuted to transportation to Australia for life. After five years the Aussie Brits thought he wasn't such a bad guy and released him on condition he never return to Ireland. He moved to Brussels, and a couple of years later he was pardoned and returned to Ireland. By then he'd had his fill of rebellion and quietly slipped out of sight. He died in 1864. He has a prominent statue but most Dubs couldn't point it out, despite it being in the middle of O'Connell Street.

Thomas Francis Meagher was also captured, tried for sedition and sentenced to be hanged, drawn and quartered. There was international outcry at the sentence, particularly as the rebellion had fizzled out. So the British, not wanting to seem like bad guys, commuted the sentence to transportation. But after

Australian prison security

two years he escaped and legged it to America where he received a hero's welcome in New York. He and another ex-Young Irelander, John Mitchel, who had also escaped from Van Diemen's Land (Jaysus, their security must have been crap), started a newspaper called *The Irish Citizen*, which was rabidly anti-British. Meagher joined the USA Army on the Union side during the American Civil War, in which he served as a Brigadier-General. After the war he was appointed Acting Governor of Montana, which was petitioning to become a state, and he made a major contribution to the effort. He drowned in 1867 when he fell from a steamboat into the Mississippi, and his body was never recovered. His death provoked enough conspiracy theories to rival JFK and was attributed to one of the following: he was rat-arsed and toppled over the rail; the Klu Klux Klan murdered him because he was anti-slavery; political enemies from Montana assassinated him; a Confederate soldier killed him out of revenge; Native American Indians killed him for taking their land. Take your pick. There's a dramatic equestrian statue of him in Waterford in which he's charging into battle wielding a sword, and an equally dramatic equestrian one in front of the Montana State Capitol.

John Mitchel, as you've heard, also escaped from his island prison in Van Diemen's Land and hooked up with Meagher in New York to produce *The Irish Citizen*. They eventually split on the issue of slavery because Mitchel was unapologetically racist, arguing that American enslaved people were better treated than Irish peasants and, besides, negroes were 'an innately inferior race'! Which, ironically, was exactly how the British viewed the Irish. Here's his view on the matter: 'We deny that it is a crime to hold slaves, to buy slaves, to keep slaves to their work by flogging, or other needful correction.' Of course this must be viewed in the context of the age, and in the context of the age, he was a scumbag. Still, he returned to Ireland eventually and was elected as MP for Tipp, who have to this day maintained a proud record of electing extremely dodgy characters. There's a statue of him in Newry, County Down.

Charles Gavan Duffy was released from prison having missed the 1848 rebellion, and he continued to champion Irish causes. But with no sign of reform coming, he threw in the towel and headed Down Under where he had much more success. He was eventually elected Premier of Victoria, despite being portrayed as an ignorant, Catholic, bog-Irishman by the local Protestant power-mongers. He'd obviously had practice for dealing with that sort of gobshite. He was even knighted for his efforts in Oz. While there he continued to champion Irish Home Rule for afar, and worked to better the living conditions of Australia's working class and farmers. He eventually retired to the south of France and although in his seventies, he still must have had a spark of life in him because he married a youngwan, named Louise Hall, and fathered four children. Fair play to you, Charlie! He died in Nice, aged 86, and was buried in Glasnevin.

The Young Irelanders may have made a hames of their uprising(s), but their non-sectarian and cultural philosophy, and their nationalist fervour made a huge impact on the as yet unborn lads who would take up the baton of Irish freedom.

ISAAC BUTT

(1813–1879)

O k, his name always provokes titters from Americans, particularly when they happen upon the Liffey bridge named in his honour, but Isaac is well deserving of that honour, as he was the first politician in Ireland to seriously suggest the notion of Home Rule. But, ironically, in his early years he was a champion of the union with Britain.

Hey everyone! My Dad's called Butt.

VOTE BUTT

Born in Glenfin in Donegal, the son of a Protestant rector, he went to Trinity at 15 and was a prof, no less, by 23. The following year he married Elizabeth Swanzy who provided him with eight children. Various mistresses also produced numerous illegitimate children and occasionally one of them would remind him of that fact by heckling him when he was making a speech. But besides being a naughty boy, Isaac was also a lawyer, a novelist, a member of the Irish Conservative Party and an Orangeman, who considered Daniel O'Connell (P162) to be a few cans short of a six-pack.

But then along came the Great Famine, and the scales suddenly fell from Isaac's eyes. When he saw the British government's gargantuan indifference to the deaths of hundreds of thousands of men, women and children, he suddenly switched lanes, realising that only an Irish parliament could have properly dealt with the situation. So one minute he was an Orangeman, the next he was supporting the Young Irelanders (P186), and he actually defended Fenians in court after the 1848 Rising.

Isaac was an MP for 30 years representing Youghal and Limerick. After the second disastrous rising of

1867, he realised that the only way to end the cycle of wojus British administration followed by wojusly planned rebellion, was to have an Irish government. He founded the Irish Home Government Association in 1870, later to become the Home Rule League, which managed to have 59 MPs elected – it was the first time Irish Home Rule had a serious, united voice in the House of Commons. One of those who joined his fledgling party was an ambitious youngfella from Wicklow called Parnell. Unfortunately for Isaac, his gentlemanly conduct in parliament was met with gentlemanly indifference by English MPs and the party was largely ignored.

The party became famous in this era for its practice of obstructionism, which was the delaying of parliamentary business by long-winded speechifying. Butt opposed this tactic, but he was getting on a bit and had to give way to energetic younger members, Parnell included, who were impatient to give the Brits a good kick up the arse. Eventually, his health failing, he gave up the leadership of the party he'd founded. He was replaced briefly by William Shaw, who would himself be replaced by Parnell the following year.

He died in 1879 and was buried in Stranolar in his native Donegal under a tree where he used to while away the hours as a young lad. There is an Isaac Butt Heritage Centre near Ballybofey, Donegal, as well as the famous Butt Bridge on the River Liffey.

THOMAS D'ARCY MCGEE

(1825–1868)

Funny one this, as D'Arcy McGee, as he was known, was more of a famous Canadian than a famous Irishman – in fact many Dubs think D'Arcy McGee's is just a well-known pub in Tallaght.

He was born in Carlingford in Louth and had his little head filled up with Irish history by his mother. The family moved to Wexford where his education continued in a hedge school. He was top of his hedge in almost every subject, and at 17 emigrated to the USA, who were always on the lookout for a gifted young Irishman. The spotty youth soon got a job on

The Boston Pilot newspaper and O'Connell (P162), no less, called his demands for the repeal of the union with Britain the 'inspired utterances of an exiled Irish boy.'

With such a reference in his pocket, he returned to Dublin where he strolled into jobs in *The Freeman's Journal* and then *The Nation*, where he could slag the British endlessly and get paid for it. By the time the 1848 rebellion came around he'd been arrested for same. He was soon released, and didn't take further part in the rebellion, but was deemed guilty by association. So he disguised himself as a priest (hard to spot one in amongst all the others), and legged it back to America.

After opening a couple of newspapers in New York and Boston, D'Arcy McGee upped sticks again in 1857 to head for Canada, where he tried his hand as a politician – and turned out to be surprisingly effective. Before long he was clambering up the political ladder. He was elected to the Canadian Parliament, with not a little help from Irish voters, and proved to be a powerful orator. He was appointed minister in several governments and campaigned like a mad thing for religious rights, non-sectarian politics, modernisation, the development of industry and of an independent Canadian culture and literature, educational rights for minorities – in fact the socially liberal Canada of today owes him a big debt. The present-day Dominion of Canada is largely D'Arcy McGee's doing, but he wouldn't be around to see its first steps as an independent nation.

Ironically, one of the few groups that couldn't stand his guts was the militant Canadian-Irish Fenians. Somewhere along the way, D'Arcy McGee had a change of heart regarding violent insurrection as advocated by Fenians, and said: 'Secret societies are like what the farmers in Ireland used to say of scotch grass. It must be cut out by the roots and burnt into

Up the rebels!

Up the royals

powder.' This upset the Canadian Fenians a bit. Well, actually, a lot. Returning from a debate in Parliament late one night, he was shot in the head by a Fenian sympathiser called Patrick Whelan, although Whelan always insisted he was an innocent scapegoat. Whelan was hanged for this crime in front of a crowd of 5000 enthusiastic Canadians, the last public hanging in the country.

D'Arcy McGee's funeral procession attracted almost all of Montreal's population. He has monuments, statues and buildings in his honour all over Canada, and a statue of him stands on Parliament Hill in Ottowa. In Ireland there are monuments to him in Carlingford, Donegal and Wexford. Pity we lost him to Canada though. Who knows what he might have achieved if he'd stayed? Still, if you're ever in D'Arcy McGee's pub in Tallaght, at least you can bore the arse off your friends by telling them all about the guy who gave the place its name.

JAMES STEPHENS

(1825–1901)

After the disaster of the 1848 rebellion, there was chaos among Irish republicans. Its supporters were spread all over the shop – America, Europe, Ballygo-backwards – and the authorities were now seriously on their guard. Along came James Stephens, who solved the problem by creating a secret, oath-bound organisation called the Irish Republican Brotherhood (IRB).

Stephens was born in Kilkenny, a smart lad who always had his nose in a book. His first calling was not blowing up things, however, but building them; he was apprenticed as a railway engineer and helped build the Limerick and north Waterford railway in the 1840s. But James was also making tracks for a life as a rebel.

The fact that he called Daniel O'Connell a 'wind-bag' gives a hint of his revolutionary leanings, and he took up arms to assist the Young Irelanders in the 1848 rebellion i.e. skirmish in Tipp. In an early indication of the covert methods he'd later use, he arranged for a local newspaper to report that he'd been killed in the fight. With the British assuming he was six feet under, he made an easy escape to Paris. There he hooked up with other exiled Young Irelanders and they spent years honing a new set of skills in Paris's flourishing underground – and we're not talking about the Metro. The city was full of French radical types and secret societies, and Stephens became skilled in the techniques of conspiracy and covert revolution.

In 1856 he was back in Ireland disguised as a tramp. And tramp he did, travelling 3000 miles around Ireland recruiting for his new secret army. By 1858 he was in Dublin and on Paddy's Day he arranged a meeting of his top brass in Lombard Street, near Trinity College, where he launched the IRB, the scourge of the British for the next 50 years. Each man took a lifelong oath to basically obey

orders and keep
his mouth shut.
Among those they
would later recruit
were O'Dono-
van Rossa (P211)
and John Devoy
(P217). The organ-
isation was run
on military lines
and Stephens was
known as its 'Head
Centre'. Before long there was an American branch,
which was handy, as that was where all the dosh for
weapons came from.

How would you like to be a Fenian, kid?

In 1861, Stephens opened *The Irish People*
newspaper in Ireland, which didn't pull its punches
regarding its views on Britain. In hindsight, having
its own publication may have been a mistake for a
secret society, as it was like holding up a sign saying
'Secret Rebel Society Hiding Here in This Building'.
Meanwhile the American arm of the IRB was planning
another rising in 1865. It dispatched the plans to Ste-

phens, but in a colossal blunder, the gob-shite courier lost them at Kings-town railway sta-tion. Sure enough the not-so-secret offices of *The Irish People* were raided, and most of its employees

arrested, tried and imprisoned, including Stephens, who was thrown into Richmond Gaol, Dublin. But the IRB still had plenty of tricks up its sleeve, and soon John Devoy used them to help Stephens escape, and flee to New York.

But there were divisions in the American IRB, who wanted to stage the next rising in Ireland. Stephens kept postponing it, because he believed they weren't ready. The eejits should have listened to him, as they clearly hadn't learned the lessons of 1848. Stephens was deposed as 'Head Centre' replaced by a Thomas J Kelly who led the Rising in 1867 to an unmitigated disaster.

Stephens' influence faded and he spent his remaining years moving between Paris, Belgium and New York, working as a journalist and supporting the republican cause. He finally returned to the ould sod in 1891, thanks to a public subscription raised by Parnell (P226) and ended his days in seclusion in Blackrock, Dublin. His funeral in Glasnevin was a huge do, attended by all the IRB top brass, including those who'd kicked him out. He'd never fulfilled his dream of leading a rising, but the organisation he'd founded would soon be at the forefront of the most famous Rising of them all.

JEREMIAH
O'DONOVAN ROSSA

(1831–1915)

O'Donovan Rossa may have been a well-known Fenian, but really, his fame was only assured by a rousing speech delivered on his behalf after he'd kicked the bucket.

Born in Rosscarbery, Cork, to tenant farmer parents, the Famine struck when he was a teenager and among its victims was his own father. He never believed the oul' guff about the Famine being an 'act of God'; he blamed the British and the experience embittered him against them to his dying day.

He married Nora Eager in 1853, they had four children, and he became a shopkeeper in Skibbereen. In between selling turnips and parsnips, he established The Phoenix National and Literary Society, whose aim was 'the liberation of Ireland by force of arms', rather than debating Shakespeare. The name came from Jerry's wish to see Ireland rise from the ashes, phoenix-like, and kick some British arses. The organisation was eventually merged with the IRB, and Jerry along with it.

Joining the IRB brought the beady eyes of the British onto him; they arrested him in 1858 and, without bothering with the inconvenience of a trial, threw him into the clink for a year. Sadly, he was widowed soon after his release. He married one Ellen Buckley, who would bear him a fifth son, but he was widowed again within two years. He married for the third time the following year, a lass named Mary Jane Irwin, who bore 13 children, giving Jerry a whopping 18 nippers all together – enough for a hurling team, including three subs. Jerry certainly had ammo in his rifle.

In 1865, by which time he was one of the IRB's leaders, he was arrested for plotting a rebellion (of 1867), found guilty of treason and sentenced to life

imprisonment. He claimed the cruel treatment he received in London's Pentonville prison included having his hands cuffed behind him at mealtimes so that he was forced to eat like a dog.

The British then decided that all these Fenian prisoner boyos were too damned expensive to keep, and they were offered exile in America if they swore not to return to Ireland for 20 years. So Jeremiah and four others were sent packing on board the SS *Cuba*, earning them the nickname 'The Cuba Five'.

But a mere ocean couldn't separate Jerry from his mission and barely off the boat, he joined the republican organisations Clan na Gael and the IRB (USA branch), and he started a newspaper called *The United Irishmen*. He also organised a 'Skirmishing Fund' – a euphemism for 'bombing fund'. This raised a huge amount of money, which financed a dynamite campaign in English cities throughout the 1880s, and which, tragically, managed to blow up a seven-year-old boy in Manchester.

The campaign struck terror into the British and made Jerry an international figure, *The New York Times* dubbing him Jeremiah 'O'Dynamite' Rossa. The British demanded his extradition, ironic really, as they'd paid his fare to the USA in the first place, but American politicians weren't keen to lose all those lovely Irish votes, so told the Brits to feck off. Perhaps it was as well Jerry stayed stateside, since his bombing campaign wasn't universally welcomed by nationalists at home, especially as Parnell was making great strides towards Home Rule.

He was almost bumped off himself in 1885, when an Englishwoman called Yseult Dudley shot him near Broadway. A dastardly British assassination attempt? O'Donovan Rossa thought so, but the British denied it, and the woman was later determined to be a few cans short of a six pack, i.e. a nutter.

In his later years, as he indulged increasingly in a whiskey or 10, his health declined. Eventually he ended up in a Staten Island hospital, where he finally cashed in his chips in 1915.

However, Jerry's biggest contribution to the cause of Irish independence was yet to come. Back in Ireland the boys, especially Pearse and Connolly, realised the value that a dead, heroic, exiled patriot could have in the run-up to the planned Easter Rising. His body was whisked back to Ireland for a ginormous funeral in Glasnevin. Pearse gave the graveside oration at Jerry's farewell bash – one of the most famous nationalist speeches in Irish history. Here's a bit of it:

'They think that they have pacified Ireland. They think that they have purchased half of us and intimidated the other half. They think that they have foreseen everything, think that they have provided against everything; but, the fools, the fools, the fools! – They have left us our Fenian dead, and while Ireland holds these graves, Ireland unfree shall never be at peace!'

There's a memorial to O'Donovan Rossa in St. Stephen's Green and a Liffey bridge named after him, not mention multiple streets and GAA clubs. And you can visit his grave in Glasnevin, where a guy dressed as Pearse delivers the famous speech daily, just in case you need your latent republican fervour whipped up.

JOHN DEVOY

(1842–1928)

Born on a tiny farm in Kildare just a couple of years before the Famine, John had a very early opportunity to appreciate the munificence of British rule – watching his neighbours starve to death all around him might, just might, have had an influence on his life as a militant Fenian.

When the family moved to Dublin, Devoy was educated by the Christian Brothers, who along with the maths and geography, religiously encouraged him to create bloody mayhem for the British. At 19 he travelled to France where he was introduced to John Mitchel (P186), no stranger to bloody mayhem himself.

Devoy took a breather from all the Irish rebel stuff to join the French Foreign Legion in 1861, giving him a chance to refine his military skills and

He joined to forget... but couldn't.

self-discipline. He saw action in Algeria before returning to Ireland – and no sooner had he stepped off the
boat than he was sworn into the IRB.

Young John proved to be a man of many talents.
He was an intelligent, energetic and persuasive young
lad, qualities which, in 1865, caused James Stephens
(P207) to appoint him Chief Organiser of the Fenians
in the British Army in Ireland, which was a big title for
a 23-year-old. Basically he persuaded Irish guys in
the regular British Army to desert, and remember to
bring their guns with them. He was very successful in
this, certainly in terms of commitments he received,
and later claimed he would have the support of 8000
trained soldiers. That same year he also orchestrated
Stephens' escape from Richmond Gaol.

But in 1866, the British cottoned on to his activities and arrested him, sentencing him to 14 years
in the slammer for treason. He was granted early
release after four years but exiled to America, where
he received an address of welcome from the House
of Representatives, a huge honour, and probably
also won some senator a few votes from the massive
Irish community.

In 1873 he joined Clan na Gael, a sister organisation of the IRB, and quickly became one of its most influential leaders. Clan na Gael was the principal provider of the spondulicks for Fenian activity. And in 1875, Devoy persuaded it to finance the amazing rescue of six Fenian prisoners from a penal colony in Fremantle, Australia, using a ship called *The Catalpa* and enough intrigue to fill a John le Carré spy novel. The men escaped to New York to massive triumphal celebrations, and John Devoy became a household name.

Devoy and Clan na Gael helped to get a few new Gaelic institutions on their feet that you might have heard of, like the GAA, the Gaelic League and the Irish Volunteers. In 1878, he showed his tactical flexibility when he initiated what became known as the 'New Departure'. This involved working with Parliamentarians, chiefly Parnell, in bringing about land reform, and it was during this period that the famous strategy of 'Boycotting' came into its own. Devoy helped to organise a largely peaceable strategy of agrarian agitation, boycotts and demonstrations that helped to change the landscape, literally and metaphorically, of Irish land ownership. Sure enough, a few of his friends in the Fenian movement didn't appreciate this pacifist stuff and carried on business as usual, i.e. murdering landlords. But kudos goes to Devoy who can truly be credited with large-scale land reform.

Devoy was kept abreast of the forthcoming Easter Rising, and despite his advancing years (he was 73 in 1915) he was keen to do his bit. When O'Donovan Rossa (P211) died that year, he was the main mover in getting the old patriot's body to Ireland, spotting the huge propaganda potential, which Pearse exploited to the full. Under his leadership, Clan na Gael also smuggled guns, ammunition and cash into Ireland for the coming storm. He even personally oversaw a meeting with German diplomats and Roger Casement (P272) in an effort to get them to send us nice German weapons. And when the Rising finally came, he tried desperately to travel so he could actually fight, but he couldn't get clearance papers in time.

He lived long enough to see Ireland win independence in 1922, and he supported the Pro-Treaty side in the Civil War. His final public appearance was when he returned in 1924 as an honoured guest of the new state. He finally surrendered to old age in New York in 1928, but was brought back to Ireland and given a military funeral with full honours in Glasnevin. There is a memorial to him near his birthplace, on the road between Kill and Johnstown.

MICHAEL DAVITT

(1846–1906)

~

Considering the bloody nature of Irish history, it's probably not surprising that few of our historical figures would have been role models for Mahatma Gandhi. Michael Davitt can be considered an exception.

At the height of the Great Famine in Mayo, the Davitt family were evicted from their cottage. Michael was five. Rather than go to the workhouse, his mother fled with the kids to Haslingden in Lancashire. But things weren't exactly a bed of roses there, and Michael had to go work in a mill, aged just nine. There were no safety measures for workers – regardless of age – and while still a child, Michael caught his right arm in industrial machinery, and had to have it amputated. And the compensation from the factory fat cats?

A grand total of zilch. With experiences such as these piling up before he was even a teenager, a career in the rebellion trade looked inevitable. But he did have one lucky break. A local English benefactor, John Dean, recognised the lad had potential and helped to fund his schooling. Later as an adult, he took classes in the local Mechanics Institute whose library provided him with an education in Irish history, land-lordism and socialism.

Aged 19 he joined the local branch of the IRB and soon became its sec-retary i.e. typing letters, smuggling arms, arranging prison breaks etc. But eventually the long arm of the law caught

Handcuff him, Jones.

up with the one-armed rebel and he was sentenced to 15 years in prison. His brutal treatment there was repeatedly raised in the House of Commons, and such a fuss was kicked up by his supporters that the British released him after seven years. He immediately rejoined the IRB and went off to America to lecture and fundraise with John Devoy (P217). His most frequent assertion was that Irish tenant farmers could never improve their lot unless they booted the landlords out and took back the land.

The year 1879 was a big one for Michael. Back in his home county of Mayo by then, he'd come to believe that violence was self-defeating and had started along the path of parliamentary politics. In April that year he organised a huge rally at Irishtown, attended by 10,000 tenant farmers, which resulted in a campaign of non-payment of rent against a local landlord, which was effective, forcing the gouger to reduce rents and stop evictions. In October he founded the Irish National Land League, which eventually won tenant farmers the right to own their land again, centuries after it was nicked by the British.

Possibly what Michael is most famous for is his campaign of passive resistance that started with the ostracising of a land agent called Charles Boycott. The campaign was a huge success and gave the English language a new word. (The word 'boycott' was actually the idea of the village of Neale's local parish priest, Fr. John O'Malley.)

Despite his rejection of violence, Michael still managed to land in jail – this time for making seditious speeches in 1881. Elected MP for Meath in 1882, he couldn't take his seat at first since he was occupying one in a prison cell. When he was released later that year he began to broaden his horizons, campaigning for many issues, such as industrial workers' rights, including those in Britain, having had first-hand knowledge, so to speak, of the conditions.

In the mid-1880s he embarked on a tour of America, Australia, New Zealand, South Africa, South America and Russia, lecturing on social and civil rights, worker's rights, universal suffrage and anti-semitism. And he even found time to tie the knot, marrying one Mary Yore of Michigan, who would furnish him with five snappers.

He and Parnell (P226) fell out over land reformation – Michael wanted to nationalise it all whereas Parnell supported a 'peasant proprietorship'. He would ultimately vote with the anti-Parnellites when the Kitty O'Shea scandal caused the Irish Parliamentary Party rift.

In 1891, he started the Irish Democratic Labour Federation to campaign for free education, reduced working hours and better pay. He was again elected MP in 1892 and 1895, and was one of the founding members of the British Labour Party. He worked tirelessly on behalf of farmers and working men everywhere, including Scotland, where he was given the unique honour of laying the first sod of turf in Celtic Park in 1892 (although it didn't matter to Michael which foot you kicked with). In his later years he wrote several valuable works documenting the times he lived in, most notably *The Fall of Feudalism in Ireland*, and *Leaves from a Prison Diary*.

He died at the age of 60 in Dublin of septic poisoning after having a tooth extracted. Some 20,000 people filed past his coffin. A huge crowd also attended his funeral at Straide in Mayo, where there is now a statue of him and a museum commemorating his life. There's another statue of him in Haslingden in Lancashire, where he lived as a child. He's also got streets and parks named after him in Mayo, Dublin, California, Boston, Michigan, Tipperary, Laois and tons of other places. And surely no-one is more deserving.

CHARLES STEWART PARNELL

(1846–1891)

~

KATHERINE (KITTY) O'SHEA

(1846–1921)

~

To use a footballing metaphor, think of Parnell as the Lionel Messi or Pele of his time, a world star, one of the most admired and skilled players on the international stage. But of course, even Pele was capable of scoring a wojus own goal in the last minute.

Considering he became a fervent nationalist and champion of the downtrodden, Parnell's background might leave you scratching your head. He was born in Avondale, Wicklow, into a gentrified Protestant family with a history of friendship with the Catholic clergy, and reputation for treating their tenant farmers like human beings (as opposed to cowshite, which was the norm).

The Parnell parents sent young Charles to England for his schooling, probably because he had 10 brothers and sisters and even their mansion couldn't cope with the numbers wanting to use the jacks every morning. He was very unhappy in school but muddled through somehow and went on to Cambridge. He didn't lack brains, in fact, most of his fellow students were heads of cabbage next to him, but his father died and he inherited Avondale. This took up so much time in trying to sort out the finances and run the estate that university took a back seat.

His father and grandfather had been opposed to the Act of Union, and Parnell was equally keen to send the British packing. He also wasn't unaware that

Parnell's first day in parliament.

most of his fellow landlords hardly even troubled themselves to dirty their expensive shoes on Irish soil. So he turned his gaze to politics, and on his third attempt in 1875, was elected an MP for Isaac Butt's (P200) Home Rule League. His first year in the House of Commons was a quiet one – he basically kept his mouth shut. This was partly because he was scared shitless of public speaking and had to will himself to make speeches. He also spent that year observing the shenanigans and double dealing that went on in the Commons and realised early on that Irish issues were given only lip service – basically British MPs couldn't give a fiddler's fart about Ireland. However, all that was about to change.

Despite being a parliamentarian, he wasn't shy about sympathising with more militant nationalists, and often rubbed shoulders with leading Fenians, including John Devoy (P217). He also teamed up with more radical Home Rule MPs like John O'Connor Power from Roscommon, and devised a policy of obstructionism in the Commons to force the gobshites to pay attention. This essentially meant speaking for hours about feck all and taking up so much time that the business of the running Britain came to a standstill. The gougers suddenly realised that Mr Parnell meant business.

Great orator he may not have been, but as an organiser and tactician he was a genius. In 1877, he replaced Butt as leader of the British arm of the Home Rule League. His star was rising fast and his first big challenge loomed.

In the late 1870s, Ireland was threatened by yet another famine, brought about by poor harvests, greedy landlords and mass evictions. In 1879 Michael Davitt (P221) formed the Irish National Land League to campaign for tenant farmers' rights. Parnell and Davitt hit it off, and Parnell even persuaded militant Fenians like Devoy to agree to work with parliamentarians in the so-called 'New Departure'. For the first time in centuries, he'd managed to get all strands of nationalism kicking with the same boot instead of kicking each other. Parnell was elected president of the League and he and Davitt instigated a massive strategy of agrarian agitation, principally the use of the 'boycott' (P219). He toured the country making speeches, such as his famous one in Ennis when he encouraged tenants to treat their landlords like the 'lepers of old' i.e. shun the scumbags.

In the middle of the campaign, Parnell went on a very successful spondulicks-raising trip to America. His growing reputation even earned him a nice lunch with President Rutherford B. Hayes. While there, he famously said: '…we will not be satisfied until we have destroyed the last link which keeps Ireland bound to England.'

He returned in 1880 for the British general election bearing the nifty nickname of 'The Uncrowned King of Ireland'. The party won 63 seats, Parnell being elected for Cork, and also to the leadership of the party. Within a year, Liberal PM Gladstone was forced to introduce the first Land Act, giving massive concessions to tenant farmers. But Parnell wasn't finished.

Around this time, the seeds for his later downfall were first sown. In fact they were sown into an Englishwoman called Katherine O'Shea, nee Wood (later nicknamed 'Kitty') during a passionate, secret love affair. The problem was that Kitty was married – and to another Irish MP called Captain William O'Shea. Tut, tut. Not the done thing.

Parnell continued the land campaign, often deliberately hinting at the potential for violence from Fenians. Gladstone, despite the fine man he was, fell into the trap of solving the Irish problem by simply oppressing its leaders. Big mistake, for when Parnell was thrown into Kilmainham Gaol in 1881, he also entered the realm of martyrdom and his popularity exploded. Gladstone realised he'd banjaxed it big time and was forced to conduct negotiations through an intermediary – one William O'Shea, no less. What a tangled web we weave. The upshot was nicknamed The Kilmainham Treaty, which granted even more concessions to tenant farmers. Parnell and the other Land Leaguers were released, and he became a national hero.

Unfortunately, days after the Kilmainham Treaty, a bunch of militant nationalist nutters called 'The Invincibles' murdered the Chief Secretary for Ireland and his under-secretary in the Phoenix Park. There was shock and outrage in Britain, and Parnell struggled to convince everyone that his party had nothing to do with the atrocity. 'The Invincibles' turned out to be not very, since most of them were quickly caught and hanged. The incident made militant Fenians unpopular and they went quiet for a couple of decades, leaving Parnell's party as the sole leaders of the nationalist movement.

Parnell and Davitt's Land League ultimately won huge concessions in the form of various Land Acts, which largely returned ownership of the land to Irish farmers, and was the biggest agrarian upheaval for centuries. And the whole thing was achieved with barely a shot fired.

Somehow amidst all of this, Parnell still found time to pop round to Kitty's gaff for their liaison. And many a happy liaison was had apparently, as he fathered three children by her. Her husband knew about the affair, and had actually once challenged Parnell to a duel over it, which kind offer had been refused, as Parnell had an allergy to bullets. But according to Kitty, O'Shea got over the shock and eventually encouraged her affair, leaving him free to carry on bonking numerous mistresses, which included Kitty's own sister, Anna Caroline, and their parlourmaid, Sarah. A real Jack-the-lad was our Willie, who wanted to keep things nice and private because he was expecting an inheritance from Kitty's aunt.

By the mid-1880s the re-branded 'Irish Parliamentary Party' held the balance of power in parliament, with both the Tories and Liberals sucking up to them for support, and promising all sorts of goodies. And as a result of prolonged negotiations with Gladstone (during which Kitty acted as a go-be-tween between Parnell and Gladstone), the PM introduced the first Irish Home Rule Bill in 1886, which, unfortunately, was defeated.

The following year Parnell found himself libelled in the press, when *The Times* newspaper published a letter, supposedly from Parnell, purporting to show support for the Phoenix Park murders. The letter was proven to be a fake, written by a crackpot anti-Parnellite called Richard Pigott, the eejit having made several trademark spelling mistakes. Parnell sued and *The Times* had to pay Parnell £5000 compensation. He was welcomed back into the Commons with a standing ovation. Could anything keep the man down? Sadly, yes.

Another Home Rule Bill was on the table through 1888 and 1889, with negotiations between Parnell and Gladstone conducted in person this time. Ireland was on the brink of ruling herself for the first time in centuries. Then on Christmas Eve 1889, disaster struck…

It's funny, but we can probably blame the Easter Rising, the War of Independence and the Civil War on Kitty O'Shea's doddery old aunt Maria. Because instead of leaving all her dosh to William and Kitty O'Shea, as expected, she left it to some cousins. So Willie, now in financial shit, had no reason to stay with his erring wife, and just days – just *days* – before Home Rule was signed off, he filed for divorce and named Parnell as the 'other man'.

The scandal was enormous. Parnell was lambasted by his enemies in Britain (it was they who unfairly gave Katherine the nickname 'Kitty', a slang term for a hooker), and Gladstone came under pressure to stop dealing with him. He told the Irish Parliamentary Party that Parnell had to go – or there would be no Home Rule. Parnell resisted, and the party split. But when Parnell and Kitty married in June 1891, the Catholic Church went bonkers. Re-marriage after divorce was a mortaller and the pair were condemned from the pulpit. Parnell lost Irish support; his days were numbered.

By now, he was also suffering from an incurable kidney disease. Despite the pain of this, he continued a nationwide series of speaking engagements in all weathers, speaking out for Home Rule. But on September 30th 1891, he left Dublin for the last time and travelled to the home he shared with Kitty in Hove, Sussex. He died in her arms on October 6th 1891, aged just 45. Tragically, the Home Rule Bill died with him, and the scene was set for the revolutions of the next century.

His funeral attracted a quarter of a million people. His gravestone was a simple boulder of unhewn Wicklow granite that reads simply 'Parnell'. Kitty vanished from the public eye, but lived for another 30 years. Parnell's loyal aide-de-camp, Henry Harrison, devoted lots of time to her, during which she gave her side of the story and passionately defended Parnell. He published her account in two books in the 1930s. Kitty died in 1921 and is buried in Sussex.

Charles Stewart Parnell was described by Gladstone as 'the most remarkable person I have ever met.' Another future PM, Asquith, called him one of the four greatest men of the nineteenth century. Pearse said he was 'a flame that seared, a sword that stabbed.' A shame he was robbed from us in the dying seconds of the game.

There is a towering monument and statue to Parnell at the north end of O'Connell Street, erected in

1911, and Parnell Square is named in his memory. There is also a statue of him in Rathdrum, County Wicklow. But Ireland's never seen his like again.

LADY GREGORY

(1852–1932)

~

There's a famous tree in the grounds of Coole Park in Galway, once the home of Lady Gregory, which has carved into it the initials of Yeats, Synge, Shaw, O'Casey and a bunch of other internationally famous literary dudes. That bit of bark gives a hint of the influence Lady Gregory had on the Irish literary revival of the early 1900s.

Born Isabella Augusta Persse at Roxborough House into a loadsamoney family with a 6000-acre estate, Augusta was educated at home, as were all well-to-do girls. Her Catholic nanny used to fill little Augusta's head with all the local folklore and teach her the occasional cúpla focal. Yet she was very loyal to king and country and all that.

When she was 28 she married a complete oul' lad, Sir William Gregory, who was 35 years her senior. On the plus side, he had even more money than her own family and a mansion near Gort, and him being a 'Sir' she could now call herself 'Lady'. They honeymooned in Spain, Italy, India, Ceylon and Egypt, but maybe because Sir Willie was almost as old as the pyramids, Augusta managed to have an affair with an English poet called Wilfrid Blunt while in Egypt.

Ten years later Sir William kicked the bucket and Augusta found herself a merry widow with lots of time and money on her hands. She began expanding her mind with the help of her home's library and visited the Aran Islands, which revived her interest in the Irish language to such an extent that she organised Irish lessons at Coole House. She then turned her hand to writing, and published a load of works about local folklore. While researching Irish history, it suddenly dawned on her that the guys she'd been supporting all her life i.e. the British Crown, had been a right bunch of bastards to Ireland. Augusta had a 'road to Damascus-type' conversion from unionism to Irish republicanism.

In 1896 she met WB Yeats (P278) and a long professional collaboration ensued. They discussed their shared love of Irish folklore, history and language until the cows came home and eventually decided that Ireland needed a National Theatre to allow us to get it all off our chests through the medium of the arts. This would eventually lead, with the collaboration of JM Synge (P304) to the founding of the Abbey Theatre in 1904. By then Augusta had started writing plays and one of them, *Spreading the News*, was performed on opening night. A few years later, when *The Playboy of the Western World* caused riots,

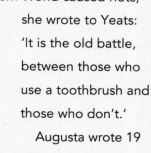

she wrote to Yeats: 'It is the old battle, between those who use a toothbrush and those who don't.'

Augusta wrote 19 plays in all, most of which were performed in the Abbey, and they were popular for a time, though not in the same category as those by Synge and O'Casey. One of her most famous works was a co-authorship with Yeats, *Cathleen ni Houlihan*. This features an old dear, Cathleen (i.e. Ireland), who owns 'four green fields' (i.e. the Provinces), asking her young men to make a blood sacrifice for her sake (i.e. take on the Brits and get blown to kingdom come). You can be sure that Pearse, Connolly, Plunkett et al were avid fans of this sort of thing.

Augusta remained an influential member of the Abbey until 1928, when she retired to Coole Park, spending her days entertaining all the literary greats of the era and getting them to autograph her tree. GB Shaw once described her as 'the greatest living Irishwoman'. She died, aged 80, at Coole Park house, which was demolished in 1941, though you can still visit the grounds and wander the paths that inspired Yeats and so many others.

SIR EDWARD CARSON

(1854–1935)

~

JAMES CRAIG

(1871–1940)

~

Most southerners imagine Edward Carson as a Paisley-like, fuming, blustering Ulsterman. But in fact he was a Dub, and only spent a tiny fraction of his life on Ulster soil.

Born in Harcourt Street to a wealthy Protestant family, he attended Wesley College and then studied law at Trinners, where he was a fellow student of Oscar Wilde, although its safe to say he found Oscar a bit 'flowery' – read on. He was fiercely loyal to Her Maj Queen Victoria, and early in his career as a prosecutor he secured many convictions against nationalists charged with violence against landlords. He was definitely not on the Fenians' Christmas card list. Not that it bothered him, as he soon earned a reputation as one of the greatest barristers of the day. In 1892 he was elected an MP for the University of Dublin and was then made British Solicitor General. The man's star was rising fast.

Then in 1895 came the trial that would be the most famous/infamous of his legal career. He was engaged to defend the Marquis of Queensberry (he of boxing rules fame) in a libel suit brought by Oscar Wilde (P248). The Marquis had made allegations of homosexuality against Oscar, a serious crime back in the day, and Oscar, foolishly as it turned out, had taken the bait. Ignoring the Queensberry Rules with which his client was associated, Carson brilliantly landed countless punches below the belt during the trial. The

case was open and shut, the Marquis having engaged private detectives to spy on Oscar's somewhat lively nocturnal activities. Oscar lost, was subsequently found guilty of homosexuality, and imprisoned with hard labour, an experience that effectively led to his untimely death.

Carson was a brilliant orator and intellect. He would use these skills in his biggest battle, which was not in the courtroom, but in public defence of Irish unionists, especially those in Ulster. For decades he'd been observing the rise of the Home Rule movement under Butt (P200), then Parnell (P226), and by the early twentieth century, John Redmond (P260), who had gotten some decent leverage with the government, was making Home Rule once again a possibility. This made Carson very, very nervous. As he saw it, if Home Rule came in, every loyal Protestant in Ireland would be royally screwed. He had no direct involvement in Ulster's politics – but that was about to change.

Meanwhile Redmond's moves on Home Rule hadn't escaped the attention of one James Craig, Ulster Unionist MP for East Down. Craig was about as orange as a ripe Seville, which has been injected with orange paint. Unlike Carson, Craig was a true Ulsterman, born in Belfast and raised in a strict Presbyterian home. As a youngfella he'd set up his own stockbroking firm and served in the Royal Irish Rifles during the Boer War. By the time he was invalided out with a dodgy eardrum, he was a master of organisation and was extremely self-disciplined. In 1906 he turned his eye to politics, and was elected as an MP.

When he observed Redmond doing deals with the British Government, his first thought was 'Home Rule is Rome Rule'; to him and his fellow Orangemen, this was like turkeys being ruled by Father Christmas. He was determined to stop the rot, but he had his limitations – he wasn't a particularly good speaker for one, and he wasn't the most famous face in Ulster. So he conceived his masterstroke – he invited Sir Edward Carson to be the figurehead in resisting the imagined Papal invasion.

Carson wasn't convinced at first, because he was unsure if they'd have enough support. Craig's answer was to rally 50,000 men to welcome Carson as their new leader, who responded with a thundering speech of the 'Ulster Says No' variety. It's a safe bet that he was an influence on the good Rev. Paisley's later style.

In 1912, Craig organised another rally in Belfast and this time invited the attendees to sign the Solemn League and Covenant of Resistance to Home Rule. Carson signed first, then Craig, and then about half a million others across Ulster. The following year they formed a provisional Ulster Government and of course when the new government required an army, 100,000 men signed up.

Craig then turned his hand to gun-running. He organised a huge delivery of weapons from Germany in 1914, which seemed very charitable of them. Of course with war looming, the sneaky Germans were happy to stir as much shit in the British Isles as they could, so they also supplied a large shipment of arms to the Irish Volunteers down south. Ireland was on the brink of a catastrophic civil war.

By this point the Third Home Rule bill ready to go. The British, realising that the Ulster lads would come in handy in the upcoming war, and that a war in their own back yard wouldn't help their cause, decided to compromise. They agreed to enact the Home Rule Bill but suspend it until after the war, after which time they'd reconsider Ulster's position. This was a victory for Carson/Craig and they assumed legendary status in the north. And as for the Home Rule Bill? It never again saw the light of day.

During WW1 Carson served as a war cabinet minister, but didn't take his eye off the ball in Ulster and continued to campaign against Home Rule. After the war, the Government of Ireland Act proposed two separate Home Rule arrangements – one for the six counties in the north and the other for the south. The south's one never happened because of the War of Independence. Carson wasn't keen but Craig embraced the arrangement like a man finding his long lost love – it was the opportunity to have a truly Protestant state free from the manky influences of Catholics.

Carson resigned as Ulster Unionist leader in 1921, and after the partition of Ireland in 1922, he repeatedly warned his former unionist colleagues, principally Craig, not to alienate Catholics, as they'd just be lighting a very long fuse. The eejits ignored his warnings, which started to become reality some 50 years later.

Carson – now Sir Edward – retired from public life in 1929 but not before witnessing the unveiling an impressive statue of himself in front of the Stormont building. He is buried in St. Anne's Cathedral in Belfast.

James Craig was appointed the first PM of the new state of Northern Ireland in 1921. In the first couple of years there was bitter Protestant-Catholic conflict, and he tried to moderate fanatical, loony, Catholic-hating bigots. But he didn't try very hard, as Catholics spent several generations as one of the most discriminated-against communities in Europe. In fact, one of Craig's bequests to his new state was to abolish proportional representation, making it virtually impossible for the minority Catholic community to elect representatives. His repeated declarations of 'Northern Ireland is a Protestant State', didn't leave much doubt about where Catholics stood. Having said that, at the same time De Valera was talking identical sectarian crap down south. So there you go.

CRAIGS
CONCENTRATED
ORANGE
BILE
100% PROTESTANT JUICE

James Craig remained as PM for almost 20 years, until his death in 1940. He died at home in Co. Down, passing away while reading a whodunnit. And as regards the mystery of who institutionalised sectarianism in Northern Ireland? Mr Craig, youdunnit.

OSCAR WILDE

(1854–1900)

W hile all the political shenanigans were afoot during the late nineteenth century, Ireland had another side that we didn't learn much about in our history books. This was the world of the arts and literature, of extravagant parties, gay soirées and cultural hedonistic pursuits. This was the world into which Oscar Wilde, playwright, novelist and poet, was born.

Although born in Westland Row, Oscar spent most of his childhood in No. 1 Merrion Square, where his eccentric mother, Jane (also a poet, known as 'Speranza'), would entertain the literati wearing gaudy, mauve dresses, several kilos of Celtic jewellery and photos of relatives dangling from various parts of her body. Little Oscar was allowed to watch these little dos, but not allowed to speak. Speranza was a Young Irelander fan who contributed poems to *The Nation*, and Irish nationalism was something with which Oscar had a lifelong sympathy. His father William, was equally 'colourful'. He was an oto-ophthalmologic surgeon (that's ear and eye doctor to you), who liked drink, ladies, and – er, archaeology.

Oscar went to school in Enniskillen, where he excelled in Greek and Roman studies, then on to Trinners and more of the same, winning the great institution's highest honours. Among his pals there was one Bram Stoker; another was Miss Florence Balcombe, with whom Oscar spent 'the two sweetest years of all my youth'. Evidently at this point the pendulum on Oscar's preferences could swing either way.

With A-grades all the way, Oscar won a scholarship to Magdalen College, Oxford, aged 20. It was here he first dabbled with writing, winning acclaim for his poem 'Ravenna.' Around now, the image of Oscar that we know and love – flamboyant dress and attitudes – was emerging from the closet, and he earned frowns from stuffy Oxford dons for strutting around with unruly hair, wearing flowers and decorating his rooms with peacock feathers. He graduated with a rare double first in Classical Moderations, and delighted in the dons' shock at 'the Bad Boy doing so well.'

After Oxford he returned to Dublin and hooked up once more with Florence, but alas, Bram Stoker had already sunk his teeth into her, metaphorically speaking, and they became engaged, breaking poor Oscar's heart. He returned to England, where he began to live the bachelor life, supported initially by an inheritance from his late father. Here he wrote his first poetry collection, called, wait for it, *Poems*. It had mixed reviews but it got his foot in the door of literary society.

By 1882, he was off to America for a lecture tour, famously remarking at the New York Customs Hall: 'I have nothing to declare but my genius.' His lectures established him as a leading advocate of the aesthetic movement (that's the pursuit of beauty for its own sake, rather than to promote a political or social viewpoint, in case you're wondering). The public adored his flamboyance and the tour was a roaring success.

Back in England in 1884, he met and married one Constance Lloyd, who would produce two children and, even in the dark days ahead, would continue to support him, well, mostly. He took a job as the editor of an ailing mag called *The Woman's World*, Ahead of his time, Oscar transformed it from a fashion magazine to one featuring women's views and feelings on social issues and literature. His editorship revolutionised the magazine's fortunes.

Around this time he wrote his only novel, *The Picture of Dorian Gray*, which shocked genteel London society, innocent things that they were. His first version had to be severely revised due to the outrage, and he edited out lots of the homo-erotic bits in particular. By now it was becoming difficult to disguise that Oscar was as gay as Christmas.

Around 1891, he met a pretty youth called Alfred Douglas, 20 years his junior. Douglas was well out of the closet and also loaded. He and Oscar fell in love immediately and Alfie introduced Oscar to the seedy underworld of Victorian male prostitution. Pretty soon their intimate relationship was an open secret and it inevitably made its way to the Marquis of Queensberry – Douglas's father.

Also around this time Oscar's creative juices started to gush, and from 1892 to 1895 he churned out play after play to critical and popular acclaim: *Lady Windermere's Fan*, *A Woman of No Importance*, *An Ideal Husband* and his masterpiece, *The Importance of Being Earnest*.

The Marquis of Queensbury confronted Oscar numerous times about the affair with his son, but the Irishman maintained it was mere gossip. Eventually the Marquis left a note in Oscar's gentleman's club addressed to 'Oscar Wilde: Posing Somdomite' (sic). His spelling wasn't the best, but the meaning was clear.

Oscar lost his rag and decided to sue Queensberry for libel – which was a bit cheeky really. Still, he knew that general knowledge of the 'crime' of homosexu-

ality would ruin him. He couldn't be dissuaded from his court action – disastrously. Queensberry hired Edward Carson (P241) to defend him and he tore Oscar to shreds on the witness stand. Oscar not only lost the libel case, but was arrested afterwards. He had a window of opportunity when he could have escaped to France, but he refused to take it. Oscar found himself in the dock, was found guilty and sentenced to two years of hard labour.

The brutality of prison pretty much destroyed him. Constance changed their children's surname to protect them from scandal, but she visited him in prison, and was the one to inform him of his mother's death. She also supported him financially in his last years.

The last thing he ever wrote was *The Ballad of Reading Gaol.* On his release, he exiled himself to Paris, pretty much destitute, and his health declined rapidly. He took to living in cheap, nasty hotels, prompting a final witticism: 'My wallpaper and I are fighting a duel to the death. One of us has to go.' A few days later, after being conditionally baptised into the Catholic church, one of the greatest aesthetes of the age lost the duel with his wallpaper. He died on November 30th 1900, aged 46.

His tomb in Père Lachaise Cemetery is a modernist masterpiece, and was recently restored – all the lipstick stains from fans were removed. Oscar also has a brilliantly colourful statue in Merrion Square, affectionately nicknamed by Dubs 'The Fag on the Crag'. But let's leave Oscar with some of his own wit: 'I am so clever that sometimes I don't understand a single word of what I am saying.'

GEORGE BERNARD SHAW

(1856–1950)

⁓

'Lack of money is the root of all evil.' One of the witty gems that flowed from the pen of another of our gazillion literary geniuses.

Born in the street later named after another of Ireland's great writers, Synge Street, Shaw wasn't fond of school, and later claimed that the standardised curricula crushed the creative spirit. But not his, obviously. His mother was a mezzo-soprano, or to put it another way, a singer, and his Da was a bit of a piss artist. His mother did a runner to London with her voice teacher when Shaw was 16 and he followed after a few years working in an estate agency.

Over the next decade he made a living as a theatre and music critic. He also wrote five novels, but after countless letters from publishers essentially telling him his work was crap, he turned to playwriting. All his novels were later published after he'd become famous.

"The problem with political jokes is that they get elected"

During this period he also became a bit of a lefty, joining the socialist Fabian Society, and a lot of Shaw's early plays are based around social inequality and hypocrisy. His work was littered with intellectual humour and caustic satire and he was also very capable of spontaneous wit. At the opening performance of *Arms and the Man* in 1894, Shaw went on stage to tumultuous applause, but when one audience member booed loudly, Shaw quipped: 'My dear fellow, I quite agree with you, but what are we two against so many?'

The following year he co-founded The London School of Economics, which is ironic really as one of his most-repeated quotes is: 'If all economists were laid end to end, they still wouldn't reach a conclusion.'

In 1896 he married Charlotte Payne-Townshend, who was a well-off Anglo-Irish woman, and they lived the rest of their days near the village of Ayot St. Lawrence in Hertfordshire, although he was a regular visitor back to the ould sod.

He churned out witty, thought-provoking plays over the next decade, including *Caesar and Cleopatra*, *Major Barbara*, *Man and Superman*, *Androcles and the Lion* and, his only play set in Ireland, *John Bull's Other Island*, which contrasted the sentimental views of Ireland's culture with the realities of life. On seeing it, King Edward VII laughed so much that he smashed his chair at the Royal Court Theatre, a snippet so widely reported that it made Shaw a household name. Publicity like that, you can't buy.

In 1912, his hugely popular *Pygmalion* gave a good slagging to the morality of the upper classes, and the play was later adapted into the film *My Fair Lady*, resulting in Shaw being the only dude ever to win, not just a Nobel Prize (1925), but also an Oscar (1938). When he was awarded the Nobel, he didn't want to know and was only persuaded to accept it by his missus, who said it would be a tribute to Ireland.

Shaw said: 'I can forgive Alfred Nobel for inventing dynamite, but only a fiend in human form could have invented the Nobel Prize.'

He rightly pissed off the British establishment during WW1, believing the whole conflict futile, and suggested that soldiers on all sides should shoot their officers. And he campaigned, fruitlessly as it transpired, against the execution of Irish rebel, Roger Casement (P272).

In 1923 he wrote what many consider his masterpiece, *Saint Joan*, about the trial of Joan of Arc, although given the subject matter, it was never going to be brimming with witty one-liners.

He spent his declining years pottering about his garden, and died at the grand old age of 94, having fallen off a ladder while pruning a bush. His ashes, and those of Charlotte, were scattered around the garden, which is now open to the public.

He was one of the greatest playwrights of the twentieth century and transformed theatre from sentimental claptrap to a place of debate on the issues of the day. Many of his plays are still regularly performed all over the world. All the Celtic Tiger bullshit would have provided him with endless material.

He left a substantial bequest to the National Gallery of Ireland, and they responded in kind with a statue of the great man in Merrion Square. There's another statue in Ontario, Canada, where an annual Shaw festival is held. His Synge Street home has also been restored and you can go and see where his rat-arsed Da drove his mother to flee abroad.

But let's finish with a Shaw quote that many Irish people will appreciate: 'Alcohol is the anaesthesia by which we endure the operation of life.'

JOHN REDMOND

(1856–1918)

~

Just like Parnell, John Redmond came within a gnat's gonad of achieving Home Rule, but a feckin' world catastrophe conspired against him. He was an odd mix – an intelligent, patriotic chap who believed passionately that Ireland should rule herself without British interference, yet also a big fan of the British Empire, and he didn't want us to sever our links completely.

Born into a family of Catholic gentry in Wexford, he studied law at Trinity (didn't everyone?) but never actually practised. He became a clerk in the House of Commons and was obviously bitten by the political bug, as he got himself elected as MP for New Ross, aged just 24. He'd remain an MP for either Wexford or Waterford pretty much for the rest of his life.

He was always a big fan of Parnell and, after the scandal, he became leader of the few remaining Parnell supporters. In 1900, he helped to re-unite many

of the estranged anti-Parnellites and the party numbers grew significantly. The Irish Parliamentary Party,
however, were about as dangerous as a toothless
puppy in the early years of the century – the Tories
were in power, supported by the Ulster Unionists, and
didn't need to give nationalists diddly squat. Things
began to seriously change after the election in 1910,
when Redmond and his party suddenly found themselves with the balance of power. Ha. Now they'd
make people listen.

Redmond negotiated with Liberal PM, Herbert
Henry Asquith, on the Third Home Rule Bill and by
1912 it was introduced into the Commons. At that
point the shit hit the fan in Ulster. Carson and Craig
(P241) mobilised a huge force of armed volunteers
to 'use all means necessary to defeat the conspiracy
to set up a Home Rule Parliament in Ireland'. With
all these armed boyos up in the north, the nationalist
Eoin MacNeill (P285) decided we'd better have our
own armed boyos, and pretty soon there were two
large armies north and south ready to obliterate each
other.

The Home Rule Bill meantime had been passed
by the House of Commons and Redmond became a

national hero, having come even closer than Parnell to a form of independence. He said: 'I personally thank God that I have lived to see this day'. But God works in mysterious ways: firstly, the Unionists used the threat of force to make Asquith amend the bill to temporarily exclude six counties in the north, and secondly, World War 1 happened. Ok, perhaps that's a theological debate for another day, but the upshot was that the bill was suspended until the end of the war.

Redmond still wasn't too put out by this, as he, and countless naïve others, thought the whole thing

would be over in a flash. So he encouraged the Irish Volunteers to sign up for the British Army in their droves as a show of loyalty to the Crown in its time of need. He truly believed their sacrifice would make the British all gooey towards us and hasten the day we'd get Home Rule. What a joke. Fifty thousand Irish lads never came home, including his own brother, Willie. On top of which, those Irish Volunteers who hadn't signed up, staged a little thing called the Easter Rising. This was a wojus blow to Home Rule. When the British decided to execute the Easter leaders, despite Redmond's pleas, national opinion suddenly swung towards militant republicanism, and at the next election his party was all but blown away by Sinn Féin.

He never lived to see that happen. Disillusioned and defeated by events largely beyond his control, he suffered a heart attack in London after a minor gallstone operation and died on March 6th 1918. His funeral service was in Westminster Abbey, but he was buried in the family vault in Wexford town.

After the nationalist fervour of the Dev years, there was sort of an unspoken decision taken to airbrush Redmond out of history in much the same way as the Soviet Union made former comrades vanish from photos, not to mention the planet. Dev and pals weren't too keen to celebrate the memory of one so fond of the Brits, despite the fact that he came within a blink of achieving Home Rule. So you won't find too many statues of him; his family vault in Wexford was so neglected that you'd have needed a machete to cut through the overgrowth. There's a monument to him in Wexford Town, but sadly, Redmond is one of the forgotten heroes of Irish history.

THOMAS J CLARKE

(1857–1916)

~

The first name on the Proclamation, Tom was also one of the main movers behind the whole shebang in 1916, and he wasn't even born in Ireland.

The honour of his birthplace goes to the Isle of Wight where he was born to Irish parents. The family later moved to Tyrone and Thomas joined the local branch of the IRB, aged just 18. When O'Donovan Rossa (P211) was orchestrating a bombing campaign in Britain, Tom was dispatched to blow up London Bridge, but was betrayed by an informer and thrown in the slammer for 15 years. Inside, he regularly had the crap kicked out of him by the guards, which he recalled in his memoir *Glimpses of an Irish Felon's Prison Life*. Not surprisingly, his loathing of the British Empire and Establishment ran deep.

When he was released in 1898, he moved to Brooklyn and married Kathleen Daly from a staunch republican family, who would later become a TD, Senator and the first female Lord Mayor of Dublin. Tom meantime took up his own republican activities with the help of John Devoy (P217) and Clan na Gael, and in 1906 bought a small farm in upstate NY, where there is now a memorial in his honour. But after just a year he and family moved back to Dublin, where he opened

Tom, maybe all this IRB stuff isn't good for our health?

a tobacconist's shop at the corner of Parnell Street and O'Connell Street (now marked by a memorial plaque). Pretty soon the IRB's top nobs like Sean Mac-Dermott (P367), Éamonn Ceannt (P348) and Bulmer Hobson (P361) were popping in for a pack of Woodbines, and Tom was up to his nostrils in IRB activities.

To Thomas, the Irish Volunteers were a potential army of liberation, so he was like a mentaller when John Redmond (P260) split the force in 1914 and the majority of the Volunteers went off to WW1 to fight for the British. Still, every cloud has a silver lining, he thought, and embraced the dictum that England's difficulty (i.e. WW1) could be Ireland's opportunity.

By now he was treasurer of the IRB and he and Sean MacDermott (P367) formed the Military Committee in 1915 to plan the following year's rising, using the remaining Volunteers. The other committee members were Pádraig Pearse P338), Éamonn Ceannt (P348) and Joseph Plunkett (P383). James Connolly (P289) also signed up early in 1916 and Thomas MacDonagh (P335) just days before the event. These were the seven who penned the Proclamation of the Irish Republic; Tom was given the honour of signing first as he was the oldest.

Come Easter Monday 1916, he was in the GPO with Pearse and Connolly, shooting at all the eejits and gougers outside. When things became hopeless he wanted to carry on to the death, but was out-voted on the matter of surrendering. He was taken to Kilmainham, court martialled and a few days later became the second person to be executed, at the age of 59. His wife Kathleen carried a message from prison: 'We believe we have struck the first successful blow for Irish freedom. The next blow, which we have no doubt Ireland will strike, will win through. In this belief, we die happy.' And six years later that turned out to be true, well, sort of.

As well as the aforementioned memorials, Dundalk's Railway Station is also named after Tom, and a couple of GAA teams. He also featured on a postage stamp. Incidentally, all of the seven signatories had one of the wojus Ballymun Flats towers named after them when they were built in 1966. Gee, thanks a bunch. Luckily they are mostly demolished now with Tom Clarke's one disappearing in a cloud of dust in 2008, thanks be to Jaysus.

DOUGLAS HYDE

(1860–1949)

Y ou know the way Irish is compulsory in school and remember the way you had it battered into ye (at least if you're over 40 you probably do), and the way you came to hate Peig Sayers' guts? Well, blame Douglas, the man largely responsible for preventing Irish being obliterated as a language, and for introducing it into the school curriculum.

But seriously, Douglas Hyde was one of the greatest cultural activists in modern Irish history, and

Comment allez vous, Schweinhund?

besides saving the language, he saved a vast amount of Irish culture from extinction.

Despite being the son of a Protestant clergyman in Roscommon, whose family had an Anglo-Irish bloodline, Douglas became interested in local folk history when young, and picked up a cúpla focal of the vanishing local dialect himself, eventually becoming fluent. He was actually a wiz at the languages in general and became fluent in Hebrew, Greek, French, Latin and German while at Trinners.

From his early thirties he put pen to paper and wrote a whole heap of books about folklore, old Irish songs, history, literature, and all in the Irish language. He was also not a bad playwright, and wrote the first ever professionally staged play in Irish, called *Casadh an tSugáin*, and in case you were asleep through all your Irish classes, that means *Turning the Straw Rope*.

But he didn't want to be a lone voice in his quest to revive Irish, so after hooking up with Eoin MacNeill (P285) in 1893, the pair founded Conradh na Gaeilge, or The Gaelic League. Within a few years it had 500 branches and pretty soon half the country was talking the talk, or ag labhairt Gaeilge. They were also dancing Irish dances, playing Irish music and listening to Irish stories and history. Douglas wrote a pamphlet entitled *The necessity for de-anglicising the Irish nation*, which would come in handy nowadays, as half the country's turned into mini-Brits, know what we mean, mate?

And as if all that wasn't enough, the Gaelic League was responsible for the national hangover that destroys one day of every year, because it was they who had St. Patrick's Day designated a national holiday. We owe Douglas a big slap on the back for that if nothing else.

The Gaelic League was founded as non-sectarian and non-political at Douglas's insistence – it was strictly cultural. But as time went by it attracted more and more fervent nationalists. Almost all the prominent leaders of the Rising would pass though its doors, and slowly they began to take the thing over. When in 1915, it was proposed and accepted that its principles include a reference to 'the pursuit of Irish freedom', Douglas resigned the presidency of the organisation he'd founded and that had achieved so much.

He returned to his day job as Professor of Irish in UCD, and disappeared from view for a decade while the nationalists and British slugged it out. He made a brief re-appearance as a senator in the new Free State in 1925, then slipped quietly away again until 1938, when Dev, in agreement with the other party leaders, proposed him as Ireland's first president, now that we were finally to become a republic. He accepted and moved into the old Viceregal Lodge in the Phoenix Park, ever since known as Áras an Uachtaráin, making his inauguration speech as Gaeilge.

His presidency was a fairly muted affair, and he generally kept his nose out of day-to-day politics. But he did come to public attention when he attended an Ireland versus Poland soccer match. The GAA hoors were outraged and removed him as their patron, forgetting all he'd done on behalf of Irish culture before most of them were out of nappies.

He continued as President until his term ended in 1945 and lived on until the fine age (especially back then) of 89. He was given a state funeral, but there was a tragic irony in the fact that the Catholic Church had banned their flock from attending Protestant services and so, with the exception of the liberally minded Noel Browne, the entire cabinet had to stand outside St. Patrick's Cathedral during the funeral service for the man who had striven to promote non-sectarianism all his life. Douglas Hyde was buried in his native Roscommon.

There are appropriately a whole heap of Irish-speaking schools named after him. And given his run-in with the GAA, there is also a nice twist in the fact that the home of Roscommon GAA is Dr Hyde Park. And of course there's the wonderful Douglas Hyde Gallery of contemporary art in the grounds of Trinity College, where he studied.

Go raibh maith agat as gach rud, a Dubhghlas.

ROGER CASEMENT

(1864–1916)

He was so, so damned British, was Roger, and he no more fits the rebel profile than a giraffe fits in a phone box. Granted, he was born in Dublin, but it was to a Captain in the British Dragoon Guards, and he was raised as a Protestant, although his mother had him secretly baptised into the Catholic Church when he was a nipper. His parents died when he was young and he was raised by relatives who were Ulster Protestants.

At 16 Roger went off to Africa and a British civil service job. He was recognised as a smart cookie with good organisational skills, and by his early thirties, he'd climbed the ladder in the consular service and was assigned to investigate human rights abuses in the Belgian Congo. This he did with great skill, his report revealing the Belgian authorities to be a bunch of greedy, murderous gougers who were systematically brutalising the locals to get rich. His report brought international action, the abuses were stopped and Roger was awarded the Order of St. Michael and St. George. A very fine, upstanding Brit, was the view of him at this point.

He returned home to Ireland on leave for a year in 1904 and took up an interest in Irish politics, supporting Arthur Griffith's (P308) newly formed party, Sinn Féin. He also joined the Gaelic League, despite only having a cúpla focal to his name.

Then the British packed him off on another consular mission to South America. Not unlike the Congo, he was assigned to investigate abuses of Peruvian locals in the rubber industry. His report in 1911 had a similar impact and won him so much admiration, the British gave him a knighthood. Step forward, Sir Roger.

But his years of tireless efforts and constant travel in the service of the British Empire had taken their toll, and he retired from the consular service back to Ireland, aged 47. Critically, he'd developed a view from his experiences in Africa and South America that empires were generally bad news for the locals and he applied the same logic to Ireland. British rule had to end.

He resumed his earlier connections with Irish nationalists, enthusiastically supported the formation of the Irish Volunteers and was appointed to the provisional committee. He went a step further the following year when he was instrumental in organising the Howth gun running. Still, his outward Britishness, his accent, his knighthood, his past, made more than a few IRB guys view him through squinted eyes. Could he be trusted?

He was in the USA raising funds when WW1 broke out and he immediately formed a plan: get the Germans on our side. John Devoy (P217) set up a meeting with the German ambassador in America and a plot was hatched. Roger set off for the Fatherland, travelling via Norway. He intended to ask the Germans to donate about 100,000 guns, as well as some officers to direct military strategy. He also planned to recruit an Irish Brigade from among Irishmen who'd been taken as POWs while fighting for the British. The last part of the plan failed completely – only a handful were willing, because in the first place the POWs had signed up to fight the Germans in defence of small countries like Belgium, and second if they joined Casement they'd be shot if the British won WW1. And unfortunately the Germans weren't willing to risk sending officers to Ireland, and were only prepared to supply 20,000 rifles that were past their sell-by date.

But to give the Germans credit, they organised the smuggling operation well – using a Norwegian vessel crewed by Germans in Norwegian uniforms and with Norwegian charts and log books etc. Unfortunately some German gobshite broadcast the operation in a communiqué to Washington and the British got wind of it.

Roger returned via submarine, which surfaced off Banna Strand in Kerry three days before the arms ship. He had to paddle ashore in a dinghy, which capsized, and he swam the rest of the way, arriving spluttering, freezing and exhausted in the early morning light. He wrote later: 'When I landed in Ireland that morning...I was happy for the first time in a year. The sandhills were full of skylarks rising in the dawn and all around were primroses and wild violets and

the singing of the skylarks in the air, and I was back in Ireland again.'

He wouldn't be happy for long. The Volunteers were supposed to meet him on Ballyheigue beach several miles away, so he spent a day and night in a ruined fort, awaiting a rescue that never came. Instead the Army turned up and arrested him, and then the Navy intercepted the ship full of weapons and scuttled the vessel.

Roger was taken to the Tower of London, tried in the Old Bailey and sentenced to death for treason. He appealed the sentence and many influential figures supported his plea, given his earlier sterling service to Britain. Among these were Arthur Conan Doyle, WB Yeats (P278) and George Bernard Shaw (P255). With the appeal pending, the authorities released Roger's diaries, which showed that his fondness for young men went far beyond brotherly love. Many believe these were forgeries, but handwriting experts now believe them to be genuine, and the debate still continues. True or not, the notion that Roger was a not only a traitor but a homosexual traitor sounded the death knell on his appeal.

Roger converted to Catholicism in his final days and Fr James Carroll attended him just before his execution. He later wrote: 'Casement was a saint, and we should be praying to him rather than for him.' He was hanged at Pentonville Prison in August 1916.

Roger Casement was initially buried in Britain, but his remains were returned to Dublin in 1965, where he lay in state, his coffin viewed by half a million people. He was given a full state funeral to Glasnevin.

There is a statue of Roger Casement at Ballyheigue in Co. Kerry, another monument to him at Banna Strand, and he has a gazillion things named after him, including GAA Clubs, housing estates, train stations and even an aerodrome.

WILLIAM BUTLER YEATS

(1865–1939)

~~~~~

It's a bit tricky to reconcile the fact that one of the greatest figures of twentieth-century literature believed in hocus-pocus, magic and related guff. But there you go. And for all we know, his poetry may have appeared from thin air after he chanted some mystical incantation.

Born in Sandymount, Dublin, into the wealthy Protestant classes, WB spent half his childhood going to school in London and the other half on holliers in Sligo. His school reports suggested he wasn't very academic and 'was very poor at spelling.' His family returned to Dublin when he was 15 and he finished his education in the Royal Hibernian Academy and the Metropolitan School of Art where he met the poet and mystic AE Russell, leading to his first real encounters with, you guessed it, poetry and mysticism. By 21 he'd decided to devote his life to writing.

He spent much of his time in the west of Ireland, where he studied Irish mythology, folklore and mysticism. WB would also become committed to the idea of an independent Ireland. Some people thought he should be committed, full stop. This was due to his membership of bodies like The Order of the Golden Dawn, which made a study of claptrap like alchemy, astral travel and geomancy. Mythology and mysticism were frequent themes of his early work and the poet

WH Auden commented on 'the deplorable spectacle of a grown man occupied with the mumbo-jumbo of magic.' Maybe, but WB's fascination with mumbo-jumbo seemed to work a spell when it came to writing poetry, and by the late 1880s he'd established himself as one of the leading poets of the day.

In 1889 he met Maud Gonne, an actress, and one of that rare breed of English people who converted heart and soul to fanatical Irish nationalism. Maud was also famous for being a bit of a babe, who could inspire any man to write love poetry. WB fell head over heels in love, but the pair didn't always see eye to eye. For one, she supported militant nationalism, whereas he thought many militant republicans were bigoted and bloodthirsty. By 1891 he'd made the first of many marriage proposals to her, which she rejected, leaving him dejected. Still, they remained close pals, and in 1902 she played the title role in *Cathleen Ni Houlihan*, the play WB co-wrote with Lady Gregory (P237). His relationship with Maud resulted in some of his greatest work, such as 'He Wishes for the Cloths of Heaven':

Had I the heavens' embroidered cloths,
Enwrought with golden and silver light,
The blue and the dim and the dark cloths
Of night and light and the half-light,
I would spread the cloths under your feet:
But I, being poor, have only my dreams;
I have spread my dreams under your feet;
Tread softly because you tread on my dreams.

Another major womanly influence on Yeats was the aforementioned Lady Gregory. They met in 1896 and, with the help of other literary types, they established the Irish Literary Theatre Society. This led to the founding of the world-famous Abbey Theatre and contributed hugely to the Irish Literary Revival, which sought to encourage Irish literature and culture so we wouldn't have to be constantly brainwashed by Brit stuff. The Abbey made Dublin one of the world's leading literary cities, although WB had to fend off riots on a couple of occasions (P239), not to mention regular criticism from both republicans and the Catholic Church.

By the turn of the century he'd put the mystical stuff behind him and much of his subsequent work was inspired by the nationalist movement, his love affairs – including one with a lady with an appropriately literary name, Olivia Shakespear – and philosophical meanderings about the meaning of life. Then in 1903, to WB's absolute horror, Maud went and married the militant republican, Major John MacBride. Her family and friends warned her it would be a disaster, and they were right. The marriage resulted in one son (Sean MacBride, who would win the Nobel Peace

Prize in 1974) and a year of unhappiness, and ended in divorce in 1905, to Yeats' relief.

He went on a lecture tour of the USA in 1903–04, and wowed the Yanks, all while churning out magnificent poetry. He and Maud finally consummated their relationship in Paris in 1908. Yeats later wrote that 'the tragedy of sexual intercourse is the perpetual virginity of the soul', whatever the hell that means. When WB told Maud how unhappy he was without her as his wife, she replied: 'Oh yes, you are, because you make beautiful poetry out of what you call your unhappiness and are happy in that,' i.e. she was doing him and the rest of the world a favour. Maybe she was.

In 1915 WB was offered a knighthood by the Britain establishment, who called him 'the English man of letters'. Typical f***ing cheek.

Along came the Rising, which resulted the execution of Maud's ex, John MacBride, and inspired work from WB, including the famous 'Easter 1916':

We know their dream; enough
To know they dreamed and are dead;
And what if excess of love

Bewildered them till they died?
I write it out in a verse—
MacDonagh and MacBride
And Connolly and Pearse
Now and in time to be,
Wherever green is worn,
Are changed, changed utterly:
A terrible beauty is born.

That same year he had better luck in the proposal stakes when he met a lady half his age called Georgie Hyde-Lees. She accepted him and they had a happy marriage, resulting in two children, although he did have the odd fling or two later in life, which Georgie knew about, and ignored.

His greatest literary height was achieved in 1923, when he became the first Irishman to win the big one – the Nobel Prize for literature.

WB was made a senator in 1922, a post he filled with distinction, although he pissed off the Catholic Church big time, for which he deserves even more accolades. He continued to churn out marvellous poetry into old age, and departed this world while on hols in France in 1939. His body was returned to his beloved Sligo after WW2 and re-interred in a simple grave in the churchyard at Drumcliff. Let's say farewell to WB with his own words, those inscribed on his tombstone:

Cast a cold eye

On life, on death.

Horseman, pass by!

EOIN MACNEILL

(1867–1945)

Some republicans hate the poor guy's guts because of one strategic decision he took in 1916, one which others argue saved thousands of lives. Hero or villain? Take your pick.

Eoin was certainly committed to nationalism and all things Irish. Born to middle-class Catholic parents in Antrim, he earned a degree and became a law clerk. But that was just the day job, as most of his energy was devoted to studying Irish culture and, together with Douglas Hyde (P268), he co-founded the Gaelic League, or Conradh na Gaeilge, which aimed to preserve the Irish language and culture, offered complete equality to women in terms of participation and administration, and, as a side-effect, brought together almost every single rebel on the island. When a proposal in 1915 included a reference to the pursuit of Irish freedom, Eoin supported it but Douglas resigned in protest.

By the early twentieth century, Eoin had become a brilliant historian and linguist, and his research into early Celtic history is still the foundation of the subject nowadays. By 1909 he was a professor at UCD.

In 1913 he wrote an article in the Gaelic League's newspaper, *An Claidheamh Soluis* (The Sword of Light) suggesting a volunteer force to protect the aspiration of Home Rule, in response to the Ulster Volunteers. The IRB jumped at the idea, having the sneaky intention of using the force to start a mass uprising. MacNeill was appointed chief of staff of the Irish Volunteers, which, in the bat of an eyelid, signed up 170,000 members.

After the split brought about by John Redmond (P260), Volunteer numbers fell to 10,000, and while Eoin MacNeill had taken to the idea of an armed uprising, he insisted they must wait until the men were fully trained and armed to the teeth, as a bunch of eejits with hurleys wouldn't advance the cause of Irish freedom much.

So he was shocked when, on Wednesday of Holy Week 1916, he learned about the planned Rising. He confronted Pearse who assured him that Roger Casement (P272) was at that moment about to deliver a gazillion German guns from a ship off Kerry. So he reluctantly agreed to get with the programme and issued orders to the Volunteers to ready themselves for 'manoeuvres'.

Unfortunately the British Navy intercepted the German ship, which the crew scuttled, sending hopes of a large-scale uprising to the bottom of the Atlantic. On Saturday, the day before the planned uprising, Eoin Mac-Neill heard the news and decided their own ship was as good as sunk. He then took one of the

most famous decisions in modern Irish history – to call off the manoeuvres. Had he not, there would have been 10,000 Volunteers fighting in the Rising, and not 1400. Fanatical republicans have never forgiven him. Less fanatical people think he was right, as even 10,000 men would have been pulverised by the massive British Army, and countless civilians killed as well. Of course the republicans argue that the rebels would have had a chance of victory, or at least inflicting serious damage on the enemy. You can argue till the cows come home.

Despite not taking part in the Rising, Eoin was sentenced to life imprisonment, although released in 1917 under the general amnesty. He stood for parliament for Sinn Féin the next year and was elected, but didn't take his seat at Westminster. He was subsequently elected to Dáil Éireann and appointed Minister for Education. He supported the 1921 Treaty, but tragically his family spilt on the issue, and his son Brian died fighting for anti-Treaty forces in 1922.

He retired from public life in his later years, but you may be interested to know (or then again you may not) that he was the granddad of former Tánaiste and Minister Michael McDowell.

JAMES CONNOLLY

(1868–1916)

~~~~

One of the legends of the Easter Rising, James was actually Scottish and an ex-British soldier. Born in Edinburgh in a right kip called Cowgate to Irish parents, his father was a labourer and his mother actually died as a result of the poverty they endured, so it was almost inevitable he'd develop lefty tendencies. The area was nicknamed 'Little Ireland', so his head was inevitably filled with Irish nationalist stuff from the word go.

His head was also deprived of any formal education, as he was sent to work in a newspaper, aged just 10. By 14, he'd had enough and lied about his age to join the British Army – the money was better and he'd get to see the world. But his postings took him only to Ireland, where he spent seven years witnessing his comrades kicking the crap out of the locals and lending backup to rich landlords. This caused a bit of a conflict of interests for him, being a devotee of Karl Marx.

While not studying socialist theory, he found time to fall in love with one Lillie Reynolds, a Protestant,

when he was posted to Dublin. When the army decided to dispatch his regiment to India, he decided the lure of Lillie was too much, and deserted. They fled to Edinburgh and married in 1890. He opened a cobbler shop, but discovered that when it came to running a business he had two left feet.

By now a fully committed socialist, he became secretary for the Scottish Socialist Federation. A fine speaker, he was invited to do a lecture tour in Scotland and America, and while in the USA he saw all the worst of the manky slum areas, and decided he needed to help his American comrades. He and family (he now had kids) emigrated there in 1903, and he naturally became involved in a gansey-load of left-wing workers' organisations. This brought him to the attention of the Irish socialist boys back home, who offered him a job as secretary of the Irish Socialist Republican Party in 1910.

The issue of workers' rights was bubbling away in Ireland at the time and, before long, Connolly was James Larkin's (P328) right-hand man in the ITGWU. In 1911, he successfully united Catholic and Protestant workers in Belfast (no small feat at the time) in the Belfast Textile Workers' strike.

In 1912 he became one of the principal founders of the Irish Labour Party. Then during the Dublin Lockout of 1913, he founded the Irish Citizen Army to help defend the workers against the Dublin Metropolitan Police, many of whom were gougers in the pay of the employers. He also gave the first hints of his growing nationalism when he founded *The Workers' Republic* newspaper i.e. not only did he want the king to feck off, he wanted the workers to run the show.

But he suspected the leadership of the Irish Volunteers weren't bothered about socialist issues – that even if they won independence they'd just be replacing one bunch of geebag capitalists with another. So he declared that he was prepared to take his Irish

Citizen Army (numbering a few hundred) into battle against the British Empire and so began marching them openly around Dublin. This scared the crap out of the IRB, then deep in the planning of the Rising, so they hastily invited Connolly to meet up, and let him in on the plan. He signed up straight away and volunteered the services of his small band.

Connolly was very influential in drafting the Proclamation of Independence, and was probably responsible for the opening words 'Irishmen and Irishwomen...', he being a supporter of feminism and egalitarianism. In fact, you'd never find a mention of women in any similar declaration in history, including the American or French version. So one nil to James. He also took the trouble to put in a word for the girls in his final dispatch from the GPO: 'Let us not forget the splendid women who have everywhere stood by us. Never had man or woman a grander cause, never was a cause more grandly served.'

During the Rising he caught a British bullet to his leg, which left him seriously injured. After the surrender he was stretchered off to a room in Dublin Castle (now called the Connolly Room), which was being used as a first-aid station, as the British wanted to save his life so that they could kill him properly later.

He was court-martialled in a wheelchair and sentenced to death. He said during his trial: 'I personally thank God that I have lived to see the day when thousands of Irish men and women were ready to affirm that truth, and to attest it with their lives if need be.' A doctor stated that James was so ill he'd be dead in two days, but the British didn't want God stealing their thunder so they decided to shoot him before the Lord could take him. Which they did, strapped to a chair, as he couldn't stand. Connolly's execution in particular made up the minds of any Irish who'd been sitting on the fence – virtually the entire country now wanted to give the British a good arse-kicking.

James Connolly was buried in Arbour Hill Cemetery, Dublin, alongside 13 other Rising leaders. Besides his tragic death in the cause of Irish freedom, he is remembered as one of the founding fathers of Irish socialism, not just in Ireland but also in Scotland. There is a statue of him outside one of Ireland's gankiest buildings, Liberty Hall (SIPTU's head office) and another of him in Union Park, Chicago, which is at least a prettier setting. He has a Dublin railway station and hospital named after him and his writings even inspired a song by John Lennon called 'Woman is the nigger of the world'. And what an irony that, in 2002, the nation who executed him voted him the 64th greatest Briton in history – funny old world.

CONSTANCE MARKIEVICZ

(1868–1927)

~

Ireland's historical hall of fame isn't exactly bulging at the seams with women because the niceties of the time decided that women didn't really have the balls to be blowing up/shooting/hacking to pieces/stabbing the ould enemy. But Constance came along like a womanly whirlwind, determined to show the guys that women could hack it, or hack up, with the best of them. She was much more than just a revolutionary though – she was also a politician, suffragette and champion of the poor.

Neither her maiden name (Constance Georgina Gore-Booth) or married name (Countess Constance Markievicz) suggested that a life as a rebel lay ahead. On top of all that she was English. Born in London to a wealthy west of Ireland landlord, Constance was raised and educated at Lissadell House, Co. Sligo, the estate where her father had provided free food to tenants during the Famine. Growing up she excelled as a horsewoman and markswoman, which would come in handy later and, because she was fair of face, was known as 'the new Irish beauty'. She was an energetic type and very intelligent, so found herself frustrated at not being allowed to vote, especially as many of the aristocratic males she encountered would have had trouble spelling 'IQ'. This prompted her to join the suffragette movement in her early twenties and participate in protests involving women chaining themselves to things and burning their bodices.

Constance was also arty, and in 1893 moved to London to study art. Five years later she moved to Paris to continue her endeavours, where she encountered a Polish painter, Count Casimir Dunin-Markievicz. They married in 1900. Casimir was bleedin' loaded and had a ginormous estate in Ukraine. After visiting it and half of Europe, they returned to Sligo in time for Constance to give birth to their only daughter, Maeve, in 1901.

But Con soon got bored mothering, left the little mite with her mother and went to Dublin. Here she began to mix with other arty and literary types in the Gaelic League, and also had her first contact with rebels. By 1908 she was a member of Sinn Féin but, amusingly, attended her first meeting in a satin ball-gown and sparkling diamond tiara, having come straight from a ball in Dublin Castle. So it took a while before she had any credibility with the lads.

By 1909, she had separated from her titled hubby, who probably didn't like the idea of his missus as a fiery rebel. The same year she and Bulmer Hobson (P361) founded Na Fianna Éireann, which was like the boy scouts except that they got merit badges for learning how to shoot things.

Not content with the rebel stuff, she took up another cause in 1911 – the plight of the poor. She worked closely with another soon-to-be rebel, James Connolly (see P289), and sold all her jewellery so she could run a free soup kitchen during the 1913 Lockout. She also joined Connolly's Irish Citizen Army and was

It's a quail and courgette consommé.

SOUP KITCHEN

made an officer – even though the notion of a woman commanding men was almost unheard of at the time. Still, they all jumped when she barked an order.

When the 1916 Rising came, she was made second-in-command to Michael Mallin in St. Stephen's Green. She demonstrated her shooting skills when she wounded a British sniper. They eventually were forced to retreat to the Royal College of Surgeons until the order to surrender came. The officer who accepted their surrender, Captain Wheeler, was actually a relative of Constance and had probably been around to her gaff for tea and biscuits. At the court martial, she was sentenced to death, but the British decided that, as they were already being seen as bloodthirsty brutes around the world, shooting a woman wouldn't improve matters, so they commuted her sentence to life imprisonment. Apparently Constance complained: 'I do wish your lot had the decency to shoot me.'

She was released under the general amnesty of 1917 but was back in the slammer in 1918 for supposedly taking part in a makey-uppy conspiracy to start another uprising, which was used as an excuse to arrest loads of Sinn Féin members. But she had the last laugh as her arrest garnered her lots of sympathy and while in prison she became the first woman ever elected to the British Parliament. When released, she became a member of the first Dáil Éireann in 1919 and was made Minister for Labour – one of the first female cabinet ministers in the world. It is a measure of how politically backward we became in the next half a century as there wouldn't be another Irish woman minister until 1979! Constance was vehemently opposed to the Anglo-Irish Treaty of 1921 and fought on the republican side in the Civil War, which earned her another trip to prison.

When Dev founded Fianna Fáil in 1926 she quickly signed up, and was duly elected in 1927. Sadly she never took up her seat as she fell ill and died five weeks after the election, probably of tuberculosis. During her funeral procession, the streets of Dublin were lined with the working-class people she'd supported all her life; Dev was one of her pall bearers and gave the funeral oration.

There's a bust of Constance in Stephen's Green and a life-size statue of her opposite Tara Street fire station. There's also a dramatic statue of her in Rathcormac, Sligo, dressed in her uniform, carrying a banner and bursting through prison gates to freedom accompanied by figures representing her various causes. Playwright Sean O'Casey said of her: 'One thing she had in abundance – physical courage; with that she was clothed as with a garment.'

ERSKINE CHILDERS

(1870–1922)

Few could have predicted that, when Erskine penned what is generally accepted to be the world's first spy thriller, he would himself become involved in international espionage.

Erskine was very, very British. Born in London to Robert Childers, a prominent civil servant, his only Irish connection was through his mother, Anna Barton, whose family were stinking rich Anglo-Irish types with a mansion in Glendalough. In fact, he was sent there as a child when his parents died, and it was there that he and his cousin, Robert Barton, would discover that they didn't like the way their lot treated the Irish.

Yet he had most of his education in British imperialist schools, and then at Cambridge, before following

Daddy's footsteps into the civil service. He became a clerk in the House of Commons, right at the heart of British rule. How far can you get from militant Irish Republicanism?

When he was 22 he volunteered to fight in the Boer War, which first gave him the impulse to write, not to mention shoot people, as he recounted in a successful book. This inspired him to write his novel *The Riddle of the Sands* in 1903, about spies, ships and skulduggery and a potential German invasion. The book was a huge success and in still in print today.

The same year, he went to the USA where he fell in love with and married Molly Osgood, whose anti-imperialist family was even richer than his own. You can gauge how wealthy her folks were from their wedding present: a 28-ton yacht called *The Asgard*. Sure beats a set of steak knives.

Erskine developed nationalist sympathies and helped to found the English Home Rule League. When the Ulster Volunteers landed arms in Larne in 1914 and the government did little to stop it, he decided to balance things up. In what could have been a chapter in his novel, he masterminded the plot to import arms from Germany and then smuggle them to Howth on board his wedding present.

Having done his bit for Irish nationalists, he then served in the Royal Navy during WW1 as an intelligence officer, planning raids on the German coast, which would have really pissed the Germans off considering they'd recently given him a shitload of guns. His service won him the Distinguished Service Cross. The ruthless suppression of the 1916 Rising and then the plans to introduce conscription to Ireland really got Erskine's goat, and when freed from military duties in 1917 he immediately returned to Glendalough.

He spent several years writing rebel pamphlets and articles, and became a close confidant of Dev. By early 1921 he was Sinn Féin's director of propaganda and that same year was elected as a TD. His nationalist cousin Robert had among his regular guests one Michael Collins, who made Erskine a gift of a gun. However, many remained wary of him, primarily because of his poncy English accent, and some even suspected he was a spy.

When the truce was called, he accompanied Griffith and Collins to London for the treaty negotiations, acting as a secretary. He was not, however, at all pleased at the outcome. He supported the anti-Treaty forces in the Civil War and secretly travelled the country bombarding people with republican pamphlets. Back at home in Glendalough in late 1922, the Free State forces caught up with him. Finding a tiny pistol, which he maintained was merely the pressy Collins had given him years earlier, he was arrested and executed at Beggar's Bush Barracks on November 24th. He took the time to shake the hands with the firing squad before he died and said: 'I die full of intense love for Ireland.'

The Asgard was restored and put on permanent display in Collins Barracks. His eldest son, also Erskine, was elected President of Ireland in 1973. Growing up posh English in Victorian Britain, it's hard to imagine that even Erskine senior would have ever seen that feckin' coming.

JOHN MILLINGTON SYNGE

(1871–1909)

~

In the recent days of austerity, our European friends were amazed at the lack of protest in Ireland. It seemed we just didn't do rioting. But that wasn't always the case, as John Millington Synge could testify.

Born in Rathfarnham, Dublin, to middle-class Protestants, John enjoyed a happy childhood despite being ill half of the time. He loved bird-watching and spent many a day wandering the Dodder River gazing at the dippers, coots and wagtails. He had an ear for an air, and could play the piano, flute and violin. But at this stage he hadn't really penned anything more than a letter to Santa Claus.

In his teens he entered Trinners, and also joined a Naturalists' club, where he developed an interest in Darwin. Reading the great man's works, he decided that the Christian version of creation was about as believable as an email from Nigeria telling you you've won the lotto. After graduating, the newly atheistic Synge decided to pursue a career as a musician and headed for Germany to study. Still no sign of any writing beyond the odd letter home to the Mammy.

He eventually abandoned the notion of music and began instead to dabble with literature, this time, in Paris. Back in Ireland by 1896, and now hovering around the edges of literary circles, he bumped into Yeats (P278), who clearly recognised some potential, and encouraged him to get down and dirty among the people of the Aran Islands.

However the following year Synge suffered his first attack of Hodgkin's Disease, which he just about survived, thanks to an operation. He decided he'd better not hang about, and took Yeats' advice to live on the Aran Islands. In fact he spent the following five summers there listening to the folklore, watching the locals at work and play, learning Irish, and having the odd pint with Mick and Biddy. Each autumn he returned to Paris much inspired. He subsequently wrote a well-regarded book called, surprise, surprise, *The Aran Islands*, in which he suggested that beneath the islanders' Catholicism was a layer of paganism.

His most famous works would all be rooted in the culture of the west of Ireland.

Meantime he'd gotten together with Yeats and Lady Gregory (P237) to form the Irish National Theatre Society, which would later establish the world-famous Abbey Theatre. And he'd also begun to pen his first serious works, including *The Shadow of the Glen*, which was on the bill on the Abbey Theatre's opening night in 1904. The play had a story about an unfaithful Irish wife, which caused an almighty furore. Arthur Griffith (P308) called it 'a slur on Irish womanhood',

because, you see, Irish women past and present are all saintly creatures without a solitary blemish on their pure white little souls. His work also got up the nose of nationalists and the church because he wasn't portraying Irish people as the honest, decent, God-fearing souls that they liked to imagine we were.

But when his masterpiece *The Playboy of the Western World* appeared, it seemed half the country were ready to burn him at the stake. First performed in the Abbey in 1907, it's a comedy set in an Irish rural pub about a man who wins the adoration of the locals for having killed his father. Politicians, the nationalist press and the church were mortified, calling it 'vile and inhuman', and 'an unmitigated libel upon Irishmen and Irish girlhood' and so on. The audience rioted on opening night and Yeats had call in the police to batter a few heads. There were repeat performances of both play and riot in New York, Philadelphia and Boston. Bunch of eejits.

Synge had certainly arrived on the stage of world literature. Sadly his appearance there would be brief. He became engaged to Abbey actress Molly Allgood that same year. But his Hodgkin's was catching up, and early in 1909, it finally brought the curtain down on him, aged 37. His work set the style for the Abbey for almost half a century and he was a huge influence on Sean O'Casey, Brendan Behan, Samuel Beckett and many others. 'Playboy' is still regularly performed around the planet.

John Millington Synge was buried in Mount Jerome Cemetery in Harold's Cross, Dublin, and his grave is sadly neglected, but its unlikely anyone's going to riot in protest. Synge Street in Dublin is named in his memory.

ARTHUR GRIFFITH

(1872–1922)

~

Like many pro-Treaty people, Arthur was pretty much erased from the history books during the Dev era, and some members of Sinn Féin even now shrink from the memory that the 'Free-Stater' was actually the one who founded their party.

Born in Dublin to a printer, he too became a printer like the Da. He scraped by, but spent most of his youth broke. So off he went to South Africa and worked in a diamond mine, and then as a journalist, in political sympathy with the Boers in their struggle against the British. He returned home in 1898 and his attention was soon transferred to the Irish nationalist struggle. He co-founded a newspaper, *The United Irishman*, which, among other things, campaigned fiercely against King Edward VII's visit in 1903.

Although he'd been a big fan of Parnell, he now decided that parliamentary participation was as useless as a chocolate teapot. He developed an alternate strategy in 1905 – the non-payment of British taxes, and Irish MPs to boycott the Commons and set up an Irish assembly. He called the strategy 'sinn féin', meaning 'ourselves'. Pretty soon the strategy became the party and Sinn Féin was born. And when *The United Irishman* was forced to close in 1906, he started a new paper called, guess what, *Sinn Féin*.

As part of his opposition to Redmond's Third Home Rule Bill and the arming of volunteers in Ulster, Arthur was one of the organisers of the Irish Volunteers and the landing of weapons at Howth in 1914. When the *Sinn Féin* newspaper called for Irish Volunteers to say a resounding 'feck off' to enlisting in the British Army in 1914, it too was closed down.

He took no part in the Easter Rising, which made nationalists raise an eyebrow or two, but he did speak in support of the rebels, earning him a trip to prison, for which he could say thanks to the British, as this made him a nationalist hero again. However, it should be pointed out before we get too excited that Arthur was also anti-semitic, especially in his younger years. He said, among other things: 'I have ... often declared that the Three Evil Influences of the century were the Pirate, the Freemason, and the Jew'. No beating around the bush there.

Before the Rising, Sinn Féin had only a smidgen of support. But after the executions there was a humungous swing in their favour and Sinn Féin virtually wiped out the Irish Parliamentary Party in the 1918 elections. Dev (P351) was appointed president with Griffith as vice president. Dev headed off to the USA for almost two years to raise money, leaving Arthur in charge; he pursued a policy of civil disobedience, with councils ignoring British directives and Sinn

Féin setting up their own judicial courts. And if that wasn't bad enough for the poor ould Brits, Michael Collins (P389) and friends started blowing them up and shooting them in a two-year-long guerrilla war. In the middle of this, Griffith was arrested and thrown into Mountjoy for eight months, but he was released in time to be nominated to go to London with Collins to negotiate the terms of the Anglo-Irish Treaty in late 1921. He wasn't that keen – he knew they would not get what they wanted. But the British negotiator, the Earl of Birkenhead, said of him: 'A braver man than Arthur Griffith, I never met'.

Back in the Dáil, Arthur argued that the agreement was a stepping stone towards full independence, but Dev and many others weren't having any of it. He resigned as president and Griffith was elected in his place in January 1922. Just six months later, banjaxed from overwork, Arthur collapsed and died, probably of a brain haemorrhage. Michael Collins attended his funeral in Glasnevin, little realising that just 10 days later he'd be back – this time permanently.

After independence, the powers-that-be tried to forget about him and his widow had to beg them for a pension. His gravestone was also a pretty paltry

Griffiths? Don't remember the fellow. Take it down, Murphy.

thing, as if they wanted to keep him out of sight. Eventually, a larger memorial would mark his resting place: a stone column seemingly with the top half missing. It was Arthur's wish – his gravestone was only to be completed when Ireland was united again. The memorial was, according to the inscription, erected not by the state, but by his loving wife, Maud. But still, there are several places named after him, including Griffith Barracks, College, Avenue and Park.

MARY MACSWINEY

(1872–1942)

~

TERENCE MACSWINEY

(1879–1920)

~

Fervent republicanism didn't so much run in the MacSwiney family as gallop. Mary would ultimately become one of Ireland's earliest and most prominent female politicians and Terence would become a nationalist martyr.

Mary was actually born in England but the family moved back to Cork when she was a nipper, and when her father legged it to Australia, her nationalist mother raised her children alone, including the toddler, Terence. Mary was a bright spark and got her teaching diploma from Cambridge University. Her mother's death in 1904 brought her home to Cork to look after her brothers and sisters, and teach school.

Little brother Terence, despite leaving school at 15 and working full time as a clerk, managed to get a degree in philosophy from UCC. His articles in the nationalist newspaper *Irish Freedom* caught the eye of the IRB, and by 1913 he was recruiting members for the Cork Brigade of the Irish Volunteers. Meanwhile Mary became a founder member of Cumann na mBan (still today listed as a terrorist group in the UK), and had clearly nailed her colours to the mast.

Terence was earmarked to be second in command of the 1916 Rising in Cork and Kerry until he stood down his forces after Eoin MacNeill's (P285) countermanding order. Yet he was arrested and packed off

to prison in Britain for a year. Mary was hauled off for 'republican activities', which at least gave the kids a free class, but also got her fired. Undeterred, she later started her own school, modelled on Pearse's St. Enda's in Dublin.

When his friend, Thomas Mac Curtain (P364), the Lord Mayor of Cork, was murdered in 1920, Terence was elected Lord Mayor himself. He was deeply embittered by British atrocities during the War of Independence and continued to preach armed resistance, which got him arrested again and sentenced to two years in Brixton prison, London. But his next act guaranteed him immortality in the republican hall of fame: Terence went on hunger strike, vowing to fast until he was released, either by the British or by death.

The hunger strike brought him to the world's attention. As it moved into weeks and then into its second month, the British ignored pleas from the USA, South America, Germany, France and Australia for his release. Terence died in October 1920 after 74 days. His graveside oration was delivered by Arthur Griffith.

Her brother's death moved Mary up from fervent to fanatical on the nationalist scale. She was one of the first women elected to the new Dáil in 1920 but was imprisoned twice during the Civil War, and bitterly opposed the Anglo-Irish Treaty in 1922. She was re-elected in 1923 but didn't take her seat. She was initially a supporter of Dev, but when he founded Fianna Fáil and moved into parliamentary politics, she and a bunch of others broke away. This left her for a time as the *de facto* leader of Sinn Féin, and arguably the first female leader of a prominent political party in Ireland.

But Sinn Féin was on the wane; Mary lost her seat in 1927 and faded slowly from the political scene. She maintained her hard-line 'not an inch' version of republicanism until her dying day.

CATHAL BRUGHA

(1874–1922)

~~~~~

It's a measure of the patriotism/fanaticism of Cathal Brugha, that despite being seriously wounded during the Rising, he ignored an order to retreat. His commander later found him, bleeding profusely, still shooting and singing 'God save Ireland'.

Born in Fairview, Dublin, to an Irish Catholic mother and an English Protestant father, he joined the Gaelic League and signed up enthusiastically to the Irish Volunteers. One of his first jobs was to organise the nationwide distribution of the Howth arms. When not smuggling weapons, Cathal indulged in sporty pastimes; he was an ace hurler, footballer and boxer.

He met his wife, Kathleen, through the Gaelic League, which seems to have doubled as a nationalist dating agency. Kathleen was also passionately republican and anti-British, and during WW2 would be accused of hiding a German spy who had parachuted into Wexford!

During the Rising, Cathal was second-in-command to Éamonn Ceannt (P348) in the South Dublin Union, and he was hit by as many as 16 bullets. While that would see most of us pushing up daisies, he battled on until the surrender was ordered. The British believed he'd croak it quickly, but he made a gradual recovery, although he'd be lame for the rest of his life.

In 1918 he was elected as a Sinn Féin MP and refused to take his seat in accordance with policy at

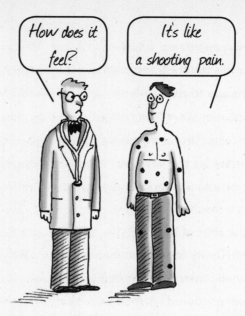

the time. The following year he was appointed Minister for Defence in the first Dáil Éireann and became Chief of Staff of the newly formed IRA. As Dev was still in the slammer in Britain, Cathal Brugha was also elected as the first President of Dáil Éireann, a post he held until Dev staged his jailbreak.

Meanwhile he developed a bitter dislike of Michael Collins (P389), who he saw as having too much influence in the IRA. He opposed Collins' tactics in the War of Independence, and dirtied his own bib when the Anglo-Irish Treaty came before the Dáil in 1922, by launching a personal attack on

Collins, questioning whether he'd ever fired a shot in Ireland's defence and claiming the British had been happy to deal with him and Griffith (P308) because they were 'the two weakest men they had on the team.' Ironically his attack may have cost the anti-Treatyites the vote, as even his own supporters were gobsmacked and several switched to Collins' side as a result.

At the start of the Civil War, Cathal was among the Anti-Treaty forces that occupied buildings in O'Connell Street. Fires forced them to retreat, and he eventually ordered his men to surrender, but wouldn't do so himself. Free State troops tried to shoot merely to wound him, but the bullet severed a major artery in his leg and he died. His body lay in state before being buried in Glasnevin Cemetery.

There is a commemorative plaque on O'Connell Street near the spot where he fell, surrounded by an artwork of 'bullet holes', and the nearby Cathal Brugha Street was named in his honour.

SIR ERNEST SHACKLETON

(1874–1922)

~

TOM CREAN

(1877–1938)

~

Irish history is littered with famous failures, most of them of the bloody rebellion type. In the case of Ernest and Tom, it was failure in the exploration department that earned them their fame, albeit a very successful failure. Confused? Read on.

Ernest was born in Kildare to an Anglo-Irish family who moved to London when he was 10, as his father was worried that nationalists might blow his brains out because of his English ancestry. Ernest was meant to follow in his father's medical footsteps, but instead, his footsteps took him into the merchant navy when he was 16. He took to the sea like a fish to water and was a master mariner by his early twenties.

His explorer's soul took him to the ends of the earth, well, not quite, but that's precisely where he intended to go: the end of the earth. The South Pole was one of the last great challenges left to human-kind and he was desperate to give it a shot. In 1901 he had his first opportunity, on board Robert Scott's Discovery expedition from 1901–1904. The expedition reached further south than ever before, and it was then that Ernest hooked up with fellow Paddy, Tom Crean.

Tom Crean was a Kerryman born to a poor farming family in Annascaul, who left school at 12 to help muck out the pigs and dip the sheep. Unsurprisingly, he'd seen enough cowshite by the time he was 15 to last a lifetime, so he joined the Royal Navy. He too had seawater in his veins, and by 22 he'd sailed the planet. While in New Zealand he volunteered to join the Discovery Expedition, where he impressed Scott, and was promoted to petty officer.

Back in warmer climates, Ernest's attempts at various business start-ups sank quicker than an anchor, and he realised the only place he could successfully stay afloat was on a ship. In 1907 he raised funding for his own expedition to Antarctica on board the

Nimrod. He didn't reach the South Pole, but broke the record for having gone furthest south, for which he was knighted. But in 1911, he had to watch in frustration as Scott set off on what would be his final attempt.

Tom Crean was on this expedition – but was left behind for the final leg of the journey, against his expectations, and the Kerryman reputedly cried with disappointment. Of course Scott had just done him a humungous favour, as a few days later they realised that the Norwegian, Roald Amundsen, had pipped them to the post, or the Pole, and then the party all froze to death on the return journey.

The South Pole having been conquered, Ernest announced that he would attempt the last great Antarctic challenge of crossing the continent from sea to sea on board the ship *Endurance*. He then placed a famous small ad in a London newspaper:

'Men wanted for hazardous journey. Low wages, bitter cold, long hours of complete darkness. Safe return doubtful. Honour and recognition in event of success.'

It sounded like a dream job to Tom Crean, and Sir Ernest signed up the Kerryman as second officer.

I warn you Crean. It will be cold, windy and inhospitable. In fact, just like Kerry.

But disaster struck when *Endurance* became stuck in pack ice and was slowly crushed. Ernest managed to guide his men to the remote Elephant Island, then he, Tom, and four others made an incredible 1300-kilometre journey in an open boat to South Georgia. For 15 days they endured violent storms, minimal rations, and sub-zero temperatures but made it to the island alive. But it wasn't over yet. Ernest, Tom and a man called Worsley then crossed 50 kilometres of rugged mountains without any proper equipment to reach a whaling station. These guys were no big girls' blouses. They returned to Elephant Island to rescue the rest of the crew – and not a single life was lost.

Although their plan to cross Antarctica had failed, their expedition is regarded as one of the greatest tales of survival in exploration history.

In 1922, while preparing for another expedition in South Georgia, Sir Ernest dropped anchor for the last time when he suffered a fatal heart, aged just 48. He was buried on the island at his wife's request.

Tom Crean meantime had moved back to Annascaul, married a local cailín and opened a pub called 'The South Pole', which is still there today. He put all his polar medals and memorabilia in a box and out of modesty, played down his own heroic achievements. Yet these were enough to earn him his own statue in Annascaul, have Mount Crean and Crean Glacier named after him, *and* get his picture on an

American beer called 'Arctica Pale Ale'! All in all, not bad for a farmer's lad from Kerry.

THE O'RAHILLY

(1875–1916)

'It is madness, but it is glorious madness!' So the man they called The O'Rahilly is reputed to have said to Countess Markievicz (P294) as the 1916 Rising began. Evidently he was well up for the fight, although he didn't believe it should have gone ahead. Sadly, the 'glorious madness' would result in him having 'KIA' after his name.

Born Michael Joseph O'Rahilly in Kerry, he grew up a fervent nationalist and was a fluent Irish speaker. At some point he granted himself the nickname 'The O'Rahilly', as though he was an ancient Irish clan chief, although it's unlikely his pals said stuff like 'D'ye fancy a pint, The?'

His family was fairly well off, and he spent lots of his own dosh supporting 'the cause'. Aged 24 he married an American cailín, Nancy Browne, who was visiting Kerry on her holliers. They went on a long honeymoon throughout Europe, during which the energetic Kerryman became fluent in French. They then emigrated New York.

A few years later the family returned to Dublin and The O'Rahilly became involved in the founding of the Volunteers. He was appointed Director of Arms, so had a leading role in the Howth arms smuggling episode. He wasn't a member of the IRB, but was a supporter of Eoin MacNeill (P285), and he had no knowledge of the forthcoming rebellion.

When MacNeill issued the order cancelling the Rising, The O'Rahilly hopped into his De Dion car, which was a classy jalopy for its time (and would itself be a victim of the Rising – burnt in a barricade) and drove with the message to Tipp, Cork, Kerry and Limerick, which resulted in the Rising being largely confined to Dublin. Arriving back exhausted, he was shocked to see the Volunteers gathering for battle, and despite being angry with Pearse, Connolly et al that they'd gone ahead despite MacNeill's orders, he immediately sprung into action. Yeats captured the moment in his poem 'The O'Rahilly': 'Because I helped wind the clock, I come to hear it strike.'

He spent the week fighting in the GPO, and on Friday of Easter week, with the building on fire, he volunteered to lead a group to establish a new base of operations in Parnell Street. Unfortunately he was caught in a burst of British machine gun fire and collapsed, seriously wounded in a doorway in what was then Sackville Lane (now O'Rahilly Parade). A Red Cross ambulance man later testified that when he discovered O'Rahilly almost a day later, he was still alive, but they were prevented from attending him by a British officer. Before he died, he managed to scribble a last letter to his wife: 'Written after I was shot. Darling Nancy, I was shot leading a rush up Moore Street and took refuge in a doorway. I got more than one bullet I think. Tons and tons of love dearie to you and the boys and to Nell and Anna. It was a good fight anyhow.'

A plaque with this text inscribed in The O'Rahilly's hand now marks the spot where he fell. He was buried in Glasnevin Cemetery.

Bit of trivia: The O'Rahilly's grandson, Ronan, was the founder of the famous sixties pirate radio station, Radio Caroline, which was broadcast from a ship. Clearly Ronan inherited some of his granddad's rebellious ways...

JIM LARKIN
(1876–1947)

WILLIAM MARTIN MURPHY
(1844–1919)

One of the longest battles in Irish history, but for once it had feck all to do with Britain. The two principal protagonists were William Martin Murphy, super-rich businessman, and 'Big Jim' Larkin, the super-poor union activist. In the end 'Big Jim' would lose, but ultimately emerge the hero, statue and all, and William would win, but end up much the poorer as he'd be viewed ever-after as the big bad witch, which was a smidgen unfair. But only a smidgen.

William was born into a comfortable world in Cork, his father owning a building business. After a private education in Dublin, he took over the Dad's business and proved to be a dab hand at it, successfully expanding it way beyond its original scope into areas like tramways. He contributed significantly to Ireland's infrastructure, building bridges, schools and churches, and employing thousands, and prided himself on treating his employees well. Most of this stuff would later be air-brushed away by those wishing to paint him as Dublin's Prince of Darkness.

At the other end of the social spectrum, Big Jim was born into squalor in Liverpool to Irish parents, and had pretty much zilch education. He was working at seven and his family's principal earner by his teens because his father had died. He naturally felt miffed at the way he and his fellow workers were treated like pack mules and rewarded only with scraps. So he joined a union and, later, the newly formed Independent Labour Party. He toiled away as a sailor and docker, and was promoted to dock foreman. He helped organise a strike in 1905, a big no-no for a foreman, and suddenly he was an ex-foreman. But he'd impressed the National Union of Dock Labourers so much with his organisational skills and oratory that they hired him and sent him to Scotland to organise workers there.

Meantime, back in Dublin, William had bought an ailing newspaper and re-launched it as what we now know as *The Irish Independent*, soon followed by *The Sunday Indo* and *Evening Herald*. He was also the main mover behind the Dublin United Tramways Company, and owned the Imperial Hotel and Clery's department store. He was a committed Home Ruler, although he felt complete independence would be bad for business. He refused a knighthood from Edward VII, as he didn't want to appear too chummy with royalty. Physically, William was a tall, skinny fella with a demeanour of perfect calm. But beneath his velvet glove was a fist of iron, with which he would flatten any eejit who got in the way of his business success. Big Jim was just about to climb into the ring.

By 1907 Larkin was in Belfast, and succeeded in unionising the docks workforce, even temporarily convincing Protestants and Catholics to stand together. The following year he successfully unionised thousands of skilled and unskilled workers in Dublin, Cork and Waterford. His charismatic presence and booming oratory was uniting the working class, and many employers became fidgety at the prospect of having to treat staff like human beings. He formed the ITGWU (which still exists as SIPTU), and started a workers' newspaper in 1911 called *The Irish Worker and People's Advocate*, which slagged the hell out of scumbag employers. A nervous William retaliated by producing his own propaganda in the *Indo*, depicting Larkin as one of the four horsemen of the apocalypse.

The unstoppable object finally met the immovable object in August 1913, after Murphy persuaded 300 employers to band together and deny work to union members. From his point of view, workers should be delighted to work 17 hours a day for crap pay and wojus conditions. What more could the ungrateful bastards want? So they locked their doors to all union members, which thanks to Larkin, was pretty much

An excellent year so far, Walsh. What could possibly go wrong now?

WILLIAM MARTIN MURPHY INC
1913

everyone. The great Dublin Lockout had begun and 100,000 workers found themselves jobless. Incidentally, one of the few large companies that didn't support the lockout was Guinness.

Dublin already had the worst slums in Europe and now starvation and disease spread though the tenements, but Murphy and pals were deaf to cries for mercy. He was soon nicknamed 'William Murder Murphy'. The month the dispute started, the Dublin Metropolitan Police baton charged a union rally in Sackville Street (O'Connell Street) and two workers were killed. The violence escalated when Murphy brought in English blackleg labour. People were forced to send their children to England to stop them starving to death.

Both sides had believed the dispute would last just weeks, but the more people suffered the more they hated the employers' guts and it dragged on through the winter and into 1914. In January, British unions refused to support Big Jim's calls for a sympathetic strike and he knew the game was up. The employers' doors opened again on January 18th and the most serious industrial dispute in Irish history, was over. Murphy had succeeded in banjaxing the union, although he hadn't eradicated it completely, and his victory was pretty temporary, as within a generation, labour unions had spread throughout Ireland's workforce and employers were forced to improve pay and conditions.

Murphy bought several buildings destroyed during the Rising and moved his newspapers' production to Abbey Street, where they stayed for 80 years. He hadn't exactly endeared himself to the general public during the strike, but when his newspaper called for the execution of James Connolly (P289) after the Rising, the masses' view of him went from gouger to traitorous geebag, although he later claimed the editorial was written without his knowledge. He died in 1919 and Dublin City Council expressed its sorrow at the passing of 'one of our ablest citizens...whose loss will be long felt by the country'. In working-class quarters his loss was long celebrated.

Big Jim was sent on a fundraising mission to the USA in 1914, and didn't come home for nine years. Having got drawn into the struggle for American workers' rights, he got himself banged up for three years for 'anarchy', and was then deported back to Ireland. He continued to campaign like a mad yoke for labour rights, and for socialist and communist policies and was eventually elected as a Labour Party deputy to the Dáil during WW2. In 1947, aged 71, he joined the great union in the sky, where he no doubt convinced the saints to strike for working conditions comparable to the angels. He was buried in Glasnevin.

Big Jim was given a fine, expressive statue in O'Connell Street, ironically just across the way from Clery's, once owned by his nemesis, which would have really put oul' William's nose out of joint. The

inscription reads: 'The great appear great because we are on our knees: Let us rise.'

THOMAS MACDONAGH

(1878–1916)

Famed revolutionary he may have ended up, but in his youth Thomas spent seven years studying for the priesthood. Well, at least he learned all about blood sacrifices, which would come in useful.

Born in Tipp to two teachers, his priestly training took place in Rockwell College. But somewhere along the way he decided that a life of celibacy was not for him and, like the Ma and Da, became a teacher. He also joined the Gaelic League, but his Irish was brutal and he hadn't a clue what was going on most of the time, pretty much like any Irish class in school nowadays. So he headed for the Aran Islands to improve his fluency, a fateful decision, for it was there he met Pádraig Pearse (P338) and the course of his life changed.

When Pearse opened St. Enda's in 1908, he signed up Thomas as a teacher, and presumably his Irish was intelligible by then, as all classes were conducted as Gaeilge. The following year he was one of the founders, along with Dev, of the Association of Secondary School Teachers, the teachers' union, which still exists. By 1910 he was tutoring Joseph Plunkett (P383), and the pair became close friends. And yet at that point Thomas actually believed in constitutional politics, and starting an armed rebellion was the last thing on his mind. But just as learned to speak fluent

336

Irish on the Aran Islands, learned to speak fluent rebel in the Gaelic League.

So Plunkett, you're saying the British ate your homework?

In 1912 he married Muriel Gifford, sister of Grace (P383) and joined the Irish Volunteers, and by 1914, he believed that Irish freedom would only be achieved with 'zealous martyrs', and was ready to be one of those if need be. In 1915 he officially joined the IRB, but despite his close relationship with Pearse, Plunkett et al, he wasn't invited on to the Military Council until almost the eve of the battle, so he didn't have a clue about what was planned. Next thing he knew he was appointed commandant of one of the strongest battalions, to be positioned at Jacob's Biscuit Factory. The British decided that the building was too difficult to assault directly, so they mostly ignored it, and the battalion didn't really see much action. When the order to surrender came, Thomas and his men were reluctant to agree and wanted to fight on, but eventually were persuaded to lay down their arms.

Thomas MacDonagh was taken to Kilmainham, court martialled and executed a few days later. Tragically, Muriel, his widow, died of a heart attack while swimming off Skerries in Dublin the following year.

Thomas was the subject of several poems by Yeats (P278) and Francis Ledwidge. There's a bust of him in the village of Golden in Tipperary, and a Thomas MacDonagh Heritage Centre in Cloughjordan, his birthplace. There are also loads of GAA clubs, a train station and even a shopping centre named after him.

PÁDRAIG PEARSE

(1879–1916)

Either a heroic nationalist or a violent head-the-ball terrorist, depending on whom you're talking to, Pádraig gets slagged a lot by history revisionists, particularly for his 'blood sacrifice' strategy. Here's the thing though: it worked.

He was a Dub, born in Great Brunswick Street, now Pearse Street. His father, James, was an Englishman but his mother, Margaret, was an Irish speaker and nationalist, who filled little Pádraig's head with Irish culture and patriotism. In his youth he loved tales of legendary Irish figures, such as Cú Chulainn, not realising he'd become a bit of a legend himself.

The jury's still out on his romantic preferences, with some maintaining Pádraig was as gay as a pink jockstrap, while others insist he was pretty straight, with just a couple of kinks. We do know that he had a close relationship with a Kerry cailín called Eveleen Nicholls, who tragically drowned when Pádraig was a youngfella. But then, in his youth, he also liked to wander Dublin's streets dressed as a woman or a beggar, ostensibly to get a closer look at the nitty gritty of life, but still, it suggests he was a teensy bit uncertain in the gender department.

By the time he was 23, he was the editor of the newspaper, *An Claidheamh Soluis* (meaning 'The Sword of Light', an early precursor to Star Wars' Light Sabre). He'd also earned a degree in modern languages at the Royal University of Ireland and studied law at King's Inns, being called to the bar in 1901.

He was rightly miffed at the way the school system seemed to be designed to turn Irish kids into little Englishmen, so he founded his own school, St. Enda's, to set things right. Initially based in Ranelagh, it eventually moved to an idyllic country estate in Rathfarnham (where the Pearse museum is now housed). The school was successful in achieving its aim of churning out lots of little Irish patriots, although it constantly teetered on the edge of bankruptcy. You can get a sense of Pádraig's mindset from St. Enda's ethos – pupils were encouraged 'to work hard for their fatherland and if it should be necessary, die for it.' And kids today think *they're* under pressure...

By 1912, he was appearing at nationalist rallies. He warned the Government that if Ireland was betrayed again (on Home Rule) 'there would be red war'. Pádraig never missed an opportunity for a bit of bloody imagery. By 1913, he was on the IRB's Supreme Council and fully supported the formation of the Irish Volunteers, seeing them as the army he hoped to lead into battle.

But in 1914, he was rightly pissed off when Home Rule was suspended and John Redmond (P260) persuaded the majority of Volunteers to fight for the British Army in WW1. Still, he was strangely delighted to see Europe thrown into violent mayhem, and saw small countries like Belgium defending their lands as very heroic, envisioning a similar slaughter in Ireland winning us world admiration. He gave us another colourful bloody metaphor: 'It is good for the world that such things should be done. The heart of the earth needed to be warmed with the red wine of the battlefields.' Appointed the Volunteers' Director of Military Organisation in 1914, Pádraig could see his battle plan slowly taking shape.

The following year he made his famous graveside oration at the funeral of O'Donovan Rossa (P211):

'They think that they have foreseen everything…
but the fools, the fools, the fools! – They have left
us our Fenian dead, and while Ireland holds these
graves, Ireland unfree shall never be at peace.'

The following Easter, he got his chance to supply
Ireland with lots more Fenian dead, as he was
appointed one of the leaders and spokesman for the
Rising. Unfortunately their plans were largely banjaxed
when the arms promised by Germany were seized by
a British ship, causing the Volunteers' Chief of Staff,
Eoin MacNeill (P285) to issue countermanding orders
to the Volunteers to stand down, which most did. This
left Pádraig and comrades with a fraction of the original numbers to go into battle. Still, all the better if he
wanted to make a blood sacrifice, as opposed to actually winning, so it was still full steam ahead.

On Easter Monday 1916, James Connolly (P289)
led the battalion that took over the General Post
Office, so it was really a bitch if you just happened
to be in posting a letter. Pádraig famously read the
Proclamation on the GPO's steps to mostly bemused
Dubs. As the week progressed and the building came
under fire, he was apparently quite calm, wandering the rooms issuing orders and offering support

to fellow rebels, though it's not known if he actually pointed his gun out of a window and took a pop at any Englishmen. When the British gunboat *Helga* bombarded the place to bits (not to mention half of Dublin) and Connolly was wounded, Pearse took command and decided to get the hell out of there. A small bunch retreated to Moore Street and held out for a while. Realising the game was up, and in order to prevent further civilian deaths, Pearse decided to surrender.

He was court-martialled at Richmond Barracks, where he exaggerated his role in the Rising and downplayed that of others, in the hope they'd be spared. But the British were itching to dispatch a few Paddies and show us who was boss, so his words fell on deaf ears. He was transferred to Kilmainham Gaol, where he wrote several letters to, among others, his mother, in which he said 'This is the death I should have asked for if God had given me the choice of all deaths'. Pádraig was executed by firing squad the following day, May 3rd, and buried in Arbour Hill Barracks.

He'd gotten his blood sacrifice, and as a result of the executions, public opinion swung massively to the nationalist side. Pádraig became a republican legend, a heroic figure who embodied Ireland, although as time progressed a lot of others stuck the boot into his reputation, calling him a terrorist and a bit of a looper with a death wish. Take your pick.

Although there are several busts of him, there's no actual Pádraig Pearse statue. Having said that you can hardly spit in Ireland without hitting something named after him – there are Pearse streets, roads, parks, schools, train stations and GAA clubs. But let's leave the last word on Pádraig to a Brit, General Charles Blackader, who presided over his court-martial:

'I have done one of the hardest tasks of my life: to condemn to death one of the finest characters I have ever come across. There must be something very wrong in the state of things that makes a man like that a rebel. I don't wonder that his pupils adored him.'

WILLIAM T COSGRAVE

(1880–1965)

W hen our newly formed state was just out of nappies, Liam, as he was known, was the man who saw us though early childhood and kept us from losing the run of ourselves, as well as providing us with some new toys, like the ESB and the Garda.

Born in James's Street, Dublin, he joined Sinn Féin and the Irish Volunteers. During the Rising, Liam served under Éamonn Ceannt (P348) in the South Dublin Union, and for his trouble was handed a death sentence, which was commuted to life imprisonment. While in prison in Wales, he was elected as an MP for Kilkenny. After his release under the 1917 amnesty, he sat in the first Dáil Éireann.

Dev made him Minister for Local Government, and he took to that like a fish to water. He set up Sinn Féin courts, which made their own rulings and passed their own sentences, much to the annoyance of the British, who found their own fancy courtrooms as empty as an Irish bank vault. He also set up assistance for the poor and organised a policy of non-cooperation with all things British, which really got on their tits, because there was little they could do about it.

Although a close confidant of Dev, he shocked the Long Fellow by supporting the Treaty of 1921. When the Free State came into being, his experience as a politician and financial know-how saw him elected as President of the Executive Council, in effect, what we now call 'Taoiseach'.

During the Civil War he made as many friends as bitter enemies. He was personally opposed to the death penalty, but his Public Safety Bill resulted in the execution of 77 anti-Treaty prisoners. He and his pro-Treaty Sinn Féiners founded a new political party called Cumann na nGaedheal, which pretty much gave Liam a free run at everything due to Sinn Féin's abstentionist policy.

In the 1920s, he and Kevin O'Higgins (P398) faced down a potential army mutiny, brought about by his decision to take an axe to the 55,000-strong army. He and O'Higgins also oversaw the formation of An Garda Síochána, or national police force, still going strong. They embarked on a radical foreign policy different to all other members of the British Commonwealth. They brought the Free State into the League of Nations and established independent diplomatic relations with foreign powers. They also set up the national radio, forerunner to RTÉ.

Liam stabilised the economy and brought our agricultural exports to heights they wouldn't reach again for decades. He established the Agricultural Credit Corporation to help farmers and also The Irish Sugar Company, which would also last until recent times, when some gobshites in the EU drove it out of existence, and then afterwards said sorry, they'd made a mistake. But perhaps Liam's government's most effective innovation was establishing the ESB, which brought light and heat to every godforsaken boreen in the back of beyond.

His government ruled for a decade until Dev's new boys, Fianna Fáil swept to power in 1932. The following year his Cumann na nGaedheal merged with other smaller parties to form Fine Gael, yet they couldn't shift Dev for 16 years, and finally Liam decided to call it a day in 1944. Although he wouldn't have admitted it at the time, many years later Dev said of Liam's government: 'They did a magnificent job…a magnificent job.'

Liam Cosgrave died in 1965, aged 85, and got a state funeral. Liam's son, also Liam, was a chip off the old block and would be Taoiseach himself from 1973 to 1977.

ÉAMONN CEANNT

(1881–1916)

~

He's probably the least known of the 1916 leaders, but Éamonn was as deserving of history's plaudits as the rest.

Born Edward Kent in Galway, his early years didn't suggest a budding republican hero in the making, as he was the son of an RIC officer, who were considered by nationalists to be slightly below pondlife. His father was transferred to Louth where Éamonn was educated by the Christian Brothers in militant nationalism. He was a real bright spark at school, getting honours in Irish, Latin, French, German, English, Arithmetic, Algebra and Drawing. He then studied at UCD and became an accountant working for Dublin Corporation.

He joined the Gaelic League in 1900, where he rubbed shoulders with Pearse (P338) and Eoin Mac-Neill (P285). Wandering around among the O'Súilleabháins and Ó'Muircheartaighs with such an English name made him feel like a naked man at a ladies knitting club, so he wisely decided to change it to Éamonn Ceannt. He joined Sinn Féin in 1907 and his adoption of republican nationalism was complete.

Éamonn was a wizard at the uilleann pipes and even established a school to promote their playing. He fell in love with Áine O'Brennan and they married in Rome in 1908, where Éamonn was invited to perform the pipes for the Pope himself. Papal blessing in his back pocket, he returned home and signed up with the IRB. He was one of the founders of the Irish Volunteers in 1913, and was assigned the job of fundraising to buy guns, his accountancy coming in handy.

I forgive you for that noise, my son.

As the planning for the Rising intensified, he was brought into the military council, many meetings taking place in his Dolphin's Barn home, a stone's throw from where he would meet his end. In the Rising itself he was Commandant of the 4th Battalion with more than 100 men under his command, and he was assigned the South Dublin Union, where St. James' Hospital now stands. He was the picture of calm as the battle raged, and the battalion held the position until the end. After the surrender, he was sent to Kilmainham, tried and executed on May 8th. His last communication was a love letter to Áine.

Galway railway station is named in his memory, as is Éamonn Ceannt Park in Crumlin, Dublin, which features a large memorial stone bearing his name.

EAMON DE VALERA

(1882–1975)

Born in the United States to a Spanish father, what were the chances Dev would become probably the most influential Irish politician in the twentieth century? Having said that, some people would prefer if he'd fecked off to Spain or stayed in America instead of adopting Ireland as his homeland.

His mother was Elizabeth Coll, from Limerick, and when Dev was two, his father died and Liz decided she'd had enough nappy-changing so sent him to be raised by his granny in Ireland. He was a brainy lad and won a scholarship to Blackrock College in Dublin. By the time he was 21, he'd been appointed professor of mathematics at Rockwell College, Tipp, which explains why he could so easily divide opinions. And it was here that his colleagues nicknamed him 'Dev'.

By then he'd already become a passionate nation-alist and lover of all things Irish, so he joined the Gaelic League. He also discovered another passion there, falling in love with his teacher, Sinéad Flana-gan. They married in 1910 and would remain so for 65 years, producing seven nippers along the way.

By 1913, Dev was a captain in the Irish Volunteers and, by 1915, a member of the IRB. During the Rising he was commandant of the battalion in Boland's Mills, and depending on whom you believe, he was either a courageous, brilliant leader or a bit of a looper. He apparently gave conflicting orders, wouldn't sleep and forgot the password so was almost shot by his own men. At one point, forced to sleep through exhaustion, he woke up screaming 'Set fire to the railway! Set fire to the railway!' After the surrender, he was sentenced to death, but later reprieved for a variety of reasons, including the fact that he was a USA citizen – the British didn't want to upset their American buddies in case they wouldn't help them out in WW1.

The Long Fellow (he was a lanky, skinny yoke) spent the following year in prison in England, and was released under the general amnesty of 1917, but was back behind bars in 1918 for protesting against Britain's decision to introduce conscription. He escaped from Lincoln Prison in 1919, returned to Ireland and was elected the President of the First Dáil Éireann. He then headed for America for a year to raise funds and to try to get official recognition for the Irish Republic. He failed in the latter, but succeeded in the former, returning with his pockets bulging with £6 million.

He landed in Ireland bang in the middle of the War of Independence, to witness Michael Collins (P389) and pals kicking the crap out of the brutal Black and Tans and the British Army. Eventually, British PM Lloyd George, decided that he'd had enough, and called for a truce. Dev decided to opt out of the negotiations that followed — many believe he pulled a fast one to avoid the blame if they failed to negotiate complete freedom. The resulting Anglo-Irish Treaty of 1921 was, unsurprisingly, not to his liking, especially the bits about the north staying in Britain and swearing an oath to the feckin' king. After the Dáil endorsed the Treaty, Dev resigned as President and Griffith was elected in his place. Dev then went on to lead the anti-Treaty forces in the Irish Civil War, eventually surrendering in May 1923.

Dev was elected to the Dáil as a Sinn Féin TD but by 1926, he'd become fed up with his party's abstentionist policy. So he formed a new party called Fianna Fáil, or the 'Soldiers of Density', sorry, 'Destiny'. Fianna Fáil's aims were a united Ireland, restoration of the Irish language, equal opportunity for all, and to make Ireland self-sufficient. All of which they failed miserably to achieve in the next 70 years. Anyway, they did well in the polls and formed a government with the Labour Party at the 1932 election. They got over their antipathy to the oath of allegiance by signing a book containing the oath, as opposed to actually saying it, which was prophetic really, as many of their later pronouncements also weren't worth the paper they were written on.

Dev's party spent much of the next 50 years in power. He introduced a new constitution, to which he allowed a humungous contribution from the right-wing Catholic Archbishop John McQuaid. He scrapped the Oath of Allegiance (points for that), and he stood down the potential coup d'état of the fascist-lite Blueshirts in 1933 (bonus points for that). Then at the end of WW2, the big long eejit offered his condolences to the German government on the death of Adolf Hitler, which banjaxed our relations with half the planet. However he did redeem himself a bit after Churchill slagged off our neutrality during the war, when he replied forcibly and to great effect in a radio broadcast.

After WW2, Dev's Fianna Fáil oversaw decades of economic stagnation and extreme Catholic conservatism, and eventually he resigned and was replaced by the great Sean Lemass. He was subsequently elected as President in 1959, where he could do little damage. He was re-elected in 1966 and finally retired in 1973. He died in August 1975 and was buried in Glasnevin after a huge state funeral. There is a statue of the Long Fellow in Ennis, Co. Clare.

JAMES JOYCE

(1882–1941)

'And whowasit youwasit propped the pot in the yard and whatinthe nameofsen lukeareyou rubbinthe sideofthe flureofthe lobbywith Shite! will you have a plateful? Tak.'

If you liked that bit of *Finnegan's Wake*, you'll love James Joyce. Of course you're probably wondering what the f*** it's all about. Well, the world's great literary minds inform us that James was arguably the greatest modernist avant-garde writer in history, so, for him, the above was nice bedtime reading material.

Born in Rathgar, Dublin, to a middle-class Catholic family, James was a swotty kid at school and a literary geek at university. He actually started out studying medicine, but in 1904, he had his first short stories published. That was also the year he met Nora Barnacle, a Galway cailín and

Joyce and Barnacle

chambermaid. They fell in love, and went on their first date on June 16th, the day that would become known to the world as Bloomsday, on which the action of his greatest novel *Ulysses* takes place.

He was fond of the gargle, it must be said, and he spent much of 1904 indulging his fondness. This led to a couple of incidents that would inspire characters in *Ulysses*. He got into a drunken mill with a guy in the Phoenix Park, and was well battered. A Jewish man called Hunter helped him home, and this chap became one of the inspirations for Leopold Bloom. He was also involved in a boozy incident in the Martello Tower in Sandycove, with the poet Oliver St. John Gogarty and another student, who fired a gun, the bullet hitting a pan over James' head. All a bit loopy, but Gogarty would be the basis for Buck Mulligan, another character in *Ulysses*. And, of course, Nora would be reincarnated as Molly Bloom.

After various run-ins with publishers, he decided to abandon Dublin, eloping with Nora. He would return only four times, although the city would be the setting for most of his works, so he obviously had some bit of a grá for the Dubs. The couple spent the next 10 years in Trieste, Italy, where they learned the local lingo. In fact James was also proficient in Gaeilge, French, basic Norwegian, German and Greek. In 1905, Nora gave birth to a son, George, to be followed in due course by a daughter, Lucia. James' brother, Stanislaus, also joined them in Trieste, mainly so he could tell James off for wasting money and being rat-arsed half the time. While in Italy James earned a meager living teaching English, so there were probably a few Italians at the time walking around and saying stuff like 'Oftwhile balbulous, mithre ahead, with goodly trowel in grasp and ivoroiled overalls which he habitacularly fondseed…'

What I actually said was 'Roger Meade's are Swiss'

James returned to Dublin in 1909 and tried to launch Dublin's first cinema – the Volta Cinematograph. It was successful until he left for Italy again, when it went bust. While in Dublin, he and Nora exchanged a bunch of quite manky letters, and Nora wasn't shy about her own desires, hoping he'd return soon and 'roger her arseways'. No wonder he wanted to get home asap.

He was back in Dublin in 1912 with his famous collection of short stories *Dubliners*. He had endless rows with his publisher, who considered it too risqué, and returned to Italy in a huff. But two years later, both *Dubliners* and his first novel, *A Portrait of the Artist as a Young Man*, finally appeared, and the critics began to realise they had a genius on their hands.

The Joyces moved to Zurich with the onset of WW1 and James began work on *Ulysses*, which took a mere seven years to knock out. But when it finally came into being, it hit a wall, and it became almost impossible to find a publisher with the guts to produce it, and probably half of them couldn't understand the feckin' thing. Finally, with the help of an American living in Paris called Sylvia Beach, *Ulysses* was published in February 1922. 'Bloomsday', the annual celebration of the novel, is when Ireland's literati and various other eejits dress up in Joycean costume and prance about town getting pissed and reciting lines from *Ulysses* to show the rest of us how ignorant we are and how intellectual they are. Not.

In his final novel, *Finnegan's Wake*, which you've already sampled, there's tons more of that incomprehensible prose just waiting to do your head in. What's it about? Who knows? Who cares? Life's too short for *Finnegan's Wake*.

The Joyces fled to the south of France to avoid the Nazi nasties in WW2, and then to Zurich, where James died on January 13th 1941, aged just 58. He was buried in Fluntern Cemetery in Zurich, the grave he now shares with Nora and son George, watched over by a statue of himself. There are gazillions of other statues, including the one in North Earl Street, Dublin, unkindly dubbed by Dubs as 'The Prick with the Stick'. There's one in the Merrion Hotel, and also in Trieste, Moscow, Zagreb, and a place called Szombathely in Hungary (work that one out!), to name but a few.

As James's himself put it in *Finnegan's Wake*:

'bababadalgharaghtakamminarronnkonnbronnton-nerronntuonnthunntrovarrhounawnskawntoohoohoor-denenthurnuk!'

BULMER HOBSON

(1883–1969)

~~~~~~

No, it's not a new kind of cider, but one of the lesser known guys behind the events of 1916. Although, like Eoin MacNeill (P285), poor Bulmer isn't top of republicans' Christmas card list.

He grew up in a Quaker home in Belfast, and his parents were liberal-minded types, his father being a Home Ruler and his mother a bit of a radical suffragette. He became interested in nationalist politics while a mere lad and joined the Gaelic League and the GAA, although at that point it might have been just to meet nice cailíns. By 18 years old, he'd become convinced that Ireland could only be freed with the use of physical force.

By 1904 he'd been sworn into the IRB and, three years later, he moved to Dublin to be closer to the heart of the action. In 1909, he and Constance Markievicz (P294) founded Na Fianna Éireann, which was a republican scouting movement, where the kids did all the usual scouty stuff like hiking, camping, weapons and explosive training etc.

He was a good co-ordinator and intelligent to boot, which the IRB appreciated, as at that stage

This badge is for bazookas, and this one is for ambushes.

the organisation was in rag order. So they promoted Bulmer to its Supreme Council in 1911 and gave him, Tom Clarke and Sean MacDermott (P367) the task of re-organising the whole shebang, which they did with great gusto. Bulmer also swore Pádraig Pearse (P338) into the IRB. The same year, 1913, he was one of the principal founders of the Irish Volunteers – iron-ically, this same organisation would be his undoing.

His star status in the IRB was dealt a deadly blow when he backed John Redmond's (P260) call on the Volunteers to fight for the British Army. By Jaysus that didn't go down well back at republican central. His close friend Tom Clarke became his distant enemy and would never speak to him again, Countess Markievicz wanted him shot and he was encouraged to resign from the IRB, encouraged as in 'Bulmer, f**k off!'

But he really got their goat come the Rising, as he was the one who rumbled that the rebellion was planned for Easter Sunday and who informed Mac-Neill, which eventually led to his famous counter-manding order, which reduced the rebel numbers by about 90%. When the IRB heard, they had Bulmer kidnapped and held him at gunpoint in a house in Phibsborough until the Rising kicked off. When the Rising started, his captors were desperate to take part, and debated executing Bulmer so they could leave, but ultimately decided to wait it out, much to Bulmer's relief.

After the Rising many republicans circulated rumours that he was a coward and a traitor, especially as he was one of the few republicans that wasn't arrested in the aftermath. However, Pearse scotched these rumours. Bulmer simply didn't believe that the Rising should have gone ahead with a wojusly short supply of weapons and training.

But his republican career was kaput, which was a shame as without his help the IRB would probably never have been able to organise any Rising at all.

After the formation of the Free State, all he could secure was a low level civil service job, and when he retired he moved first to Connemara and then to Limerick. He disappeared into obscurity and when his death was reported in 1969, many people were surprised that he'd still been alive all this time. Ironically, the same month he died, the Troubles in his native Ulster kicked off...

THOMAS MAC CURTAIN

(1884–1920)

We could always rely on the British to contribute to their own misfortune in Ireland by committing some outrage that would send gansey-loads of people flocking to become rebels. Probably their most prominent victim of the War of Independence was Thomas Mac Curtain, Lord Mayor of Cork. He wasn't a victim of war, though, but of murder.

For my next trick I will play the bagpipes and violin while reciting the sonnets of Shakespeare

Born in Ballyknockane in Cork, Thomas became a secretary in the local Gaelic League when still a teenager and also met his bride there, Eilish. They married in 1908 and went on to have six kids.

Thomas was a bit of a polymath and could wax lyrical on poetry, history, archaeology, languages and music – he was proficient with the bagpipes and the violin, though not at the same time.

He was commandant of 1000 Volunteers in Cork preparing for the 1916 Rising, but due to communication breakdown, their Rising never really, well, rose. The British surrounded his force in a hall for several days before they surrendered. Afterwards

Thomas was imprisoned in Wales for a year, but after his release he joined the Irish Republican Army, which had evolved from the remnants of the Volunteers.

In January 1920, at the height of the War of Independence, Thomas was elected as Lord Mayor of Cork. But just two months later on March 20th, his 36th birthday, a bunch of men with blackened faces burst into his home and shot the unarmed Thomas dead. It was later revealed that they'd been an RIC assassination squad led by one Inspector Oswald Swanzy, who was quickly transferred to Lisburn in Antrim to put the gouger out of harm's way. An inquest conducted by Coroner James J McCabe found the brutal murder had been carried out by the RIC under direction of the British Government and returned a verdict of wilful murder against PM Lloyd George and various other prominent politicians and policemen, including Swanzy.

Five months later, Michael Collins (P389) personally handed Thomas's own gun to one of his men, who used it to shoot Swanzy dead as he left church in Lisburn. Afterwards, there was a wave of violence against Catholics in Lisburn, who were attacked, and their homes and businesses burned or ransacked.

Thomas's murder caused countrywide outrage and numbers willing to take up the fight swelled in the immediate aftermath. Thomas's successor was Terence MacSwiney (P313) – but that's another tragic story. There is a memorial of Thomas outside Cork City Hall and Thomas Mac Curtain's GAA Club in London is named in his honour.

SEAN MACDERMOTT

(1884–1916)

Sean was one of the men responsible for organising the 1916 Rising – and another fan of the oul' blood sacrifice idea...

Born in Leitrim into a world of poverty and oppression, from his days as a spotty teen Sean had to move to Glasgow, and then to Belfast in 1902, where he first signed up with the IRB. The leadership realised that he was a smart cookie who would better serve them in the capital.

He proved a brilliant organiser, running an election campaign for Sinn Féin and co-ordinating IRB activities nationwide. The IRB was revitalised under his leadership, and young lads queued to join up as though the latest iPod had just been launched. He also managed *The Irish Freedom*, which didn't mince its words:

'Our country is run by insolent officials to whom we are nothing but people to be exploited and kept in subjection. Their power rests on armed force that preys on people with batons if they have the gall to say they don't like it.'

Sean was struck down by polio in 1912, and would require a walking stick for his few remaining years. But it didn't slow his march towards rebellion, and

in a speech in Tralee in 1914, he warned: 'The Irish patriotic spirit will die forever, unless a blood sacrifice is made in the next few years.'

By then Sean was on the IRB's Supreme Council and a close pal of Tom Clarke (P264). In 1915, he was thrown in the clink for campaigning against British Army recruitment. By the time of his release, his blood was boiling – and ready to be spilled. He was immediately appointed to the IRB's Military Committee and began to plan for mass rebellion like a man possessed.

Easter Sunday 1916 arrived and he rose ready for action. Frustrated but undeterred by the conflicting orders fiasco, he and over 1000 Volunteers held their nerve until the following day, when they went into battle. Sean spent the week in the GPO, but due to his polio affliction, couldn't participate in the fighting. He was among those who retreated to Moore Street where they were surrounded, and he voted to surrender in the hopes of sparing the lives of some of his young comrades. However, as they were being marched away, he remarked: 'The cause is lost if some of us are not shot.'

Incidentally, he was identified as one of the leaders by one Daniel Hoey of Dublin Castle's G Division,

who would later be assassinated by Michael Collins'
Squad (P389). So too would a British officer, Lee
Wilson, who ordered Sean's death. Before his execution on May 12th, Sean wrote: 'I feel happiness the like
of which I have never experienced. I die that the Irish
nation might live!'

There is a statue of Sean in his home village of
Kiltyclogher, inscribed with the above quotation.
Sean MacDermott Street in Dublin is also named after
him not to mention a gazillion railway stations, roads
and GAA clubs.

THOMAS ASHE

(1885–1917)

~

You'd have more than enough fingers on one
hand to count the rebel military successes in the
Rising. In fact your index finger and thumb would do.
The most successful of these can be attributed to
Thomas Ashe.

Born in the Gaeltacht area of Lispole, Co. Kerry, he
trained as a teacher in Waterford before becoming a

school principal in Lusk, Co. Dublin, so he had experience early on of bellowing orders. Like most republicans he became a member of the Gaelic League, and his charismatic personality and leadership qualities soon saw him on the governing committee. He was also a pretty nifty bagpipe player – he taught himself, which is a feat worthy of a statue in itself. In 1910 he founded the Black Raven Pipe Band in Lusk, which is still droning away happily more than a century later.

A founding member of the Irish Volunteers, he also joined the IRB, who decided his powerful oratorical skills would be handy in raising funds in the USA, which he successfully did in 1914. When he returned,

he got another teaching job, this time in Corduff, west Dublin, which was then in the wilds. When not teaching normal classes, he taught rebellion – secretly giving military training to locals in preparation for the battle ahead.

When the Rising came, Thomas commanded 40 volunteers operating in north Dublin and around Ashbourne, Co. Meath. They first successfully banjaxed the railway bridge into Dublin, hampering British efforts to bring reinforcements into the city. They next forced the surrender, after a shootout, of the RIC barracks in Ashbourne.

But then a group of about 70 RIC men arrived in 17 motor vehicles. Ashe quickly ordered his men to take positions along either side of the road. A firefight commenced that lasted several hours, and in north Dublin parlance, the RIC were hockeyed by half their number. The volunteers lost two men while the RIC lost 11 and had 20 wounded.

After the Rising, the unit surrendered and Thomas was sentenced to death, later commuted to life imprisonment. He was released the following year under the general amnesty but was soon behind bars again for giving a speech 'causing disaffection', which is funny, as it's not like there was any affection for the British in the first place.

What happened next though, was anything but funny. He was sentenced to two years hard labour in Mountjoy, but demanded to be treated as a political prisoner and went on hunger strike. The authorities decided to force feed him, but stuck the tube through his gullet and into his lungs instead of his stomach. He died later the same day. An inquest found the authorities' actions to be 'inhuman, dangerous and barbaric'.

Thomas's death prompted a surge in recruitment into the republican movement, which would considerably aid Michael Collins (P389) in the coming War of Independence. Thirty thousand people followed Thomas's funeral cortege to Glasnevin and the Big Fellow himself gave the oration.

There is a monument in his honour near Ashbourne and a statue near his birthplace in Kerry. The Ashe Memorial Hall in Tralee is named after him, which houses the Kerry County Museum. One piece of trivia: Thomas was a distant relative of Hollywood legend, Gregory Peck.

SEAN O'CASEY

(1886–1923)

~~~

What was it (or is it) about this country that we drove almost all our writers out of the place? Mind you, some of the goings on of our politicians, clergy and businessmen is enough to drive anyone to distraction, not to mention to France or England, and it seems it wasn't so different back in Sean O'Casey's day.

Sean O'Casey is generally said to have been born as John Casey into relative poverty. His family were Protestants living in Dorset Street, Dublin, and his father died when Sean was a snapper. As a child, he suffered from poor eyesight, but said later that 'it didn't matter, because there was nothing much to look at anyway.' He ended up educating himself, which included learning how to nick books from shops. He spent much of his youth either working 12-hour days as a railwayman, or sitting at home reading Shakespeare by candlelight.

Given the fact that he had holes in the arse of his pants much of his early life, he inevitably drifted towards socialism. He was also drawn to the cause of nationalism and joined the Gaelic League, learned Irish and how to play the uilleann pipes, and adopted the Irish version of his name. In the coming years, he also signed up to the IRB, Connolly's (P289) Irish Citizen Army and Larkin's (P328) ITGWU. Still no sign of a play at that stage. Mind you, he must have been busy.

Sean took part in the Dublin Lockout in 1913, which cost him his job, and the following year he resigned from the ICA in protest at them allowing dual membership of the Irish Volunteers – he believed the two issues of socialism and nationalism should be kept apart.

He didn't participate in the 1916 Rising, but when his friend Thomas Ashe (P370) died on hunger strike in 1917, it moved him to lift a pen and compose a couple of laments. During the next few years, he started writing plays, and submitted one to the Abbey Theatre. They rejected it, but thought it showed promise. In 1923 he submitted another play to the Abbey, and this time they jumped on it. *The Shadow of a Gunman* was a huge critical and

By the way, you know "paycock" is spelt wrong?

commercial success, and had them queuing down Abbey Street for tickets.

This play, and all of his famous trilogy of great plays, dealt with the issues of Dublin's poor and with nationalistic politics. He had another monster hit with *Juno and the Paycock* the following year, and again with *The Plough and the Stars* in 1926. The latter play really got up the noses of just about everyone, pissing off nationalists and every holy Joe in the country, because of the presence of a prostitute in one scene, the very existence of such ladies in Ireland being a thing the good Catholic people couldn't contemplate. The audience rioted, as they had in 1907 (P239), causing Yeats (P278) to cry: 'You have disgraced yourself again, is this to be the recurring celebration of the arrival of Irish genius?'

And genius he was, lauded in literary circles from New York to Sydney and everywhere in between. In

1927, in London to receive a literary award, he met a fine Irish cailín called Eileen Reynolds, whom he married and who would give him three children.

Unfortunately Sean had peaked with *The Plough and the Stars*, and when his next play *The Silver Tassie* was submitted to the Abbey, it was rejected. He was a tad annoyed, you could say, disgusted even, and decided he'd had enough of Ireland, its priests and its politics, and fled to London in 1928, never to return.

Although he wrote many fine plays in the years after, none matched the brilliance of his Dublin trilogy. Perhaps he needed a few gouger priests and gombeen politicians getting up his nose to inspire him. Or perhaps he just needed the Irish air, or the occasional Irish pub.

He lived to be a very respectable 84 and died in Torquay in 1964. He said in later life that 'It takes both courage and patience to live in Ireland'. And, Jaysus, that's still true.

HARRY BOLAND
(1887–1922)

All's fair in love and war, or so they say. But as the rival of Michael Collins (P389) in both love and war, poor Harry lost out to his one-time great friend.

He was born in Phibsborough, Dublin, into a family with deep roots in the nationalist movement and the GAA. His father died when he was eight and he went to live with relatives in Laois, who were even more nationalistic than his Da, so it was really always a one-way street for Harry. And sure enough, aged 17, he joined the IRB.

Harry was also pretty nifty with a hurley and could puck a ball with the best of them. That combined with his oratorical skills, and no small amount of charm led to him becoming a member of the Dublin County GAA Board when he was only 20. Two years later he was dispatched to London on GAA business (and a bit of rebel business), where he first met Michael Collins. He introduced the Big Fellow to Sam Maguire, who in turn introduced Mick to the IRB.

He joined the Irish Volunteers in 1913, and along with his two brothers played a part in the Easter Rising. After being arrested at the GPO he was packed off to Dartmoor where one of his fellow jailbirds was Eamon De Valera. He and Dev became thick as thieves and Harry remained a big fan.

Out of prison, he was appointed Honorary Secretary to Sinn Féin in 1917, but he needed a day job, so he opened a tailor's shop in Abbey Street.

Besides taking up the legs of trousers etc, his shop was busy stitching up British Intelligence, fronting as a meeting and information point for Collins' network of spies. In 1918, he stood for election in South Roscommon, winning in a landslide victory. That was also the year he and Michael stayed at the Greville Arms Hotel in Granard, Longford, where they both fell head-over-heels in love with Kitty Kiernan. It was a love triangle, but a kind of love détente existed, and they never came to blows over Kitty, physically or verbally.

In January 1919, Harry and Michael went to England to visit their old pal Dev who was in Lincoln Gaol, although they didn't go through normal visiting formalities. They arranged a blank key and files to be smuggled into the prison inside a cake, and this was used make keys that allowed Dev to escape through a side door, where Harry and Michael whisked him away to Dublin. Dev didn't linger long there, heading to America to raise

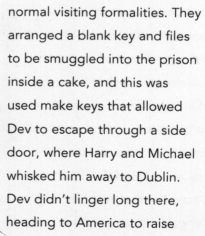

Taxi!

funds and campaign for international recognition of the new state. He also decided to bring Harry.

In the USA Harry made a huge contribution to the raising of over $5 million, worth about a gazillion in today's terms. In an interesting aside, he was also tasked with looking after the Russian Crown Jewels while there. They'd been handed over to the Irish delegation as collateral for a loan we'd given the Russian Government of $25,000. Back in Ireland, he kept the priceless objects under the floorboards in his Ma's gaff, who left them there until 1938 when she returned them to Dev's government. They were put in a safe and forgotten about until 1948. The lads considered auctioning them at that point but in the end their conscience got the better of them and they were returned to the Soviet Union in 1950 in exchange for the original sum of the loan.

Harry was back in Ireland in late 1920, and the War of Independence was in full swing. He and Michael collaborated on much of the strategy that eventually forced the truce of June 1921. Sadly, when The Big Fellow and Griffith (P308) returned from London in December that year, the Treaty was not to Harry's liking, which isn't really surprising, he having been an early convert to Dev's viewpoint. He tried desperately to find a common ground, but to no avail, and the conflict spiralled into violence and pitched brother against brother.

Harry, now identified as an anti-Treaty republican, was in The Grand Hotel in Skerries, in north Dublin, when he was shot in August 1922 by Free State soldiers supposedly while resisting arrest, although it's never been clear exactly what happened. He survived the initial attack, but died later in St. Vincent's Hospital. There's a school on the site in Skerries now, along with a commemorative plaque. His death deeply upset Michael Collins, who had but little time to grieve, as he was also assassinated just three weeks later.

Harry was buried in Glasnevin with thousands in attendance, and the scene of his burial was captured in a painting by Jack B Yeats, which is in the Sligo Public Library Collection.

Harry was portrayed by Aidan Quinn in the movie *Michael Collins*, although there was artistic licence taken which depicted Harry being shot in the River Liffey while trying to escape.

JOSEPH PLUNKETT

(1887–1916)

~

GRACE GIFFORD

(1888–1955)

~

The youngest of the seven signatories of the Proclamation, the tale of Joseph and his wife Grace's doomed love never fails to bring a tear to the eye.

Born into a well-off family on a farm in Kimmage, Dublin, Joseph's father, George, was a papal count and, and besides his devotion to the Pope, was also a devotee of nationalism. Joseph was educated first in Dublin and then sent to Stonyhurst College, England, where the British kindly provided him with military training that he would later use to shoot a bunch of them.

Joseph had the misfortune to contract tuberculosis when he was a lad, which would afflict him all his short life. A gifted poet and writer, he joined the Gaelic League and studied militant republicanism, thanks to a friendship he developed there with the rebel Thomas MacDonagh (P335). It was at the opening of Pearse's (P338) St. Enda's School in Rathfarnham in 1908 that his eye first fell upon the lovely Grace Gifford.

Grace, the child of a mixed marriage, was raised as a Protestant. Her Da was a solicitor and she grew up in a big house in Rathmines. She showed great artistic promise as a youngwan and was packed off to the Dublin Metropolitan School of Art, where she studied under the great Irish artist, William Orpen. He encouraged her talent for caricature and illustration and she eventually moved to London to develop her skills. By 1908, she was scraping a meagre living selling her cartoons to magazines, but enjoyed a bit of craic nonetheless as her work provided social contact with lots of well-known literary and arty types. Which is how she came to be invited to St. Enda's opening ceremony, and there met Joseph, the love of her life.

But first there were separations to be endured. Joseph graduated from UCD in 1909, but his TB was murder, especially in rainy, cold Dublin, so he spent a couple of years under sunny skies in Italy, Algeria and Egypt. Back in Ireland in 1912, he immediately hooked up with Connolly's (P289) and Larkin's (P328) socialists, who were then doing battle with the employers, and he campaigned on their behalf during the 1913 Lockout.

By 1914, Joseph was an influential member of the IRB, and his father provided his Kimmage farm as a distribution station for the arms that had been landed at Howth in 1914. And over the next couple of years the mooing of the cows mingled with the sounds of marching feet, as the farm became an IRB training ground for young Irish fellas who had returned from Britain to avoid conscription.

In 1915, he was dispatched to Germany to help Roger Casement (P272) persuade the Germans to part with some guns, and was the main mover in persuading them to agree – though it was a shame that his efforts proved to be in vain, as the ship was scuttled.

All this time, he and Grace had been seeing each other, and he eventually proposed and was accepted. Her sister, Muriel, had married Thomas MacDonagh in 1912. Grace converted to Catholicism just a couple of weeks before the Rising, which incidentally, she hadn't a clue was about to take place. It's reminiscent of a

Shakespearian tragedy that, while Grace was making plans for a double wedding on Easter Sunday (with yet another of her sisters and her fiancée), Joseph wasn't allowed to reveal that he'd be otherwise occupied around then, due to the absolute secrecy of the planning.

Thanks to his bit of military training, Joseph was appointed Director of Military Operations. But it was another operation that nearly scuttled his chances of taking part in the Rising – one for his glandular tuberculosis. Just days before the event, Joseph found himself confined to bed. With the help of a young unknown aide-de-camp you might have heard of called Michael Collins (P389), he was able to stagger wheezing and still bandaged to the GPO that fateful

Easter Monday, to be present at the historic event. Incidentally, that same morning his brother George also had an interesting journey. He was heading into town from Harold's Cross with over 50 volunteers. Realising they were late, he famously stopped a tram with a revolver, took out his wallet and said, 'I'd like 52 tuppenny tickets to the city centre, please.'

Despite Joseph's precarious health, he continued to direct operations for the entire week of the Rising. After the surrender, he was taken to Kilmainham, court martialled and sentenced to death. When Grace heard the news, she hurried into the city and bought a wedding ring then went straight to Kilmainham. After six hours' waiting, the British acceded to her request, and at 1 a.m. in the tiny candlelit prison chapel, and under the watchful eye of 20 soldiers with bayonets fixed (in case it was some dastardly plan to escape), Joseph and Grace were married. Joseph was immediately returned to his cell, although Grace was allowed to see him for ten minutes later that night, again in the presence of soldiers. A few hours later he was taken out and shot. Just before his execution he said: 'I am very happy I am dying for the glory of God and the honour of Ireland.'

During the Civil War, Grace joined the anti-Treaty forces, but was arrested and imprisoned in Kilmainham. While there she painted lots of murals, some of which survive, including one of the Blessed Virgin and Child, which is still a popular image for tourists to snap.

She was somewhat ostracised later for supporting the rebels in the Civil War. She struggled to get a job and was almost penniless, until Dev granted her a pension in 1932. She never remarried, and died alone in her flat in South Richmond Street in 1955, aged 67. She was buried with full military honours in Glasnevin Cemetery with President Séan T O'Kelly in attendance. A folk song called *Grace* was recorded by Jim McCann. The railway station in Waterford was named after Joseph along with the barracks in the Curragh Camp, Kildare.

MICHAEL COLLINS

(1890–1922)

~

KITTY KIERNAN

(1892–1945)

~

National heroes of legendary status require several crucial ingredients: courage, brains, vision, and good looks. Oh, and one other: you have to die young. Michael Collins ticked all these boxes. And Kitty played the supporting role of lover torn between Mick and his best friend.

Born in Sam's Cross, Cork, into a fairly well-off family, his father, also Michael, was a farmer who dabbled with mathematics. At the age of 60 he married a cailín 37 years his junior, then quickly multiplied two into a family of 10, Michael being the youngest of eight children. Not bad for an oul' lad. On his deathbed six years later, he said: 'Take care of Michael. One day he'll be a great man. He'll do great work for Ireland.' Obviously he was also a fortune-teller.

Before his first teenage spots appeared, Mick had already earned the nickname, 'The Big Fellow'.

Kitty Kiernan entered the world via Granard in Longford. Her parents owned nearly half the feckin' town – the hotel, grocery, bakery, hardware, a pub, timber yard. In fact, there was no way to escape giving them your money, as they also owned the undertakers. She enjoyed a happy upbringing until her late teens, when she lost her two sisters, and both parents. Suitors came and went but Kitty was choosy, or perhaps 'couldn't choose between them', would be more accurate.

When Michael was 15 he emigrated to London and worked in various banks and investment companies. Being on English soil didn't dilute his Irishness a smidgen, and he soon joined the local GAA club where he met the man whose name is on everyone's lips come September – Sam Maguire. By 1915 Sam had signed Michael up for a different game, recruiting him into the IRB. It was through the London GAA that he met his great friend, Harry Boland (P378) – but the pair would become rivals in love and, eventually, rivals in war.

Back in Dublin to take up a job in an accountancy firm, Mick took up a second job as Joseph Plunkett's (P383) aide-de-camp, helping in the movement of arms and drilling of volunteers ahead of the Rising. He served in the GPO under Plunkett, and after the surrender, he was shipped off to Frongoch prison in Wales. His experiences in the Rising caused him to believe they'd made a right hames of it.

The British had done the rebels a nice favour by sticking so many of them together in Frongoch, and the place was nicknamed 'The Rebel University' with Mick one of the principal lecturers. It was here he first emerged as a leader, intent on a guerrilla war. He was very athletic and competed in contests in Frongoch, winning the 100-yard dash in just over 10 seconds (the world record was 9.37 seconds!), which was useful practice as he'd be legging it a great deal in the coming years.

Michael was released in December that year, and by the following October was on Sinn Féin's executive committee. While canvassing for a by-election in Longford in 1918, he and Harry Boland stayed at The Greville Arms Hotel in Granard, owned by Kitty

Kiernan's family. There the pair temporarily forgot the by-election and began canvassing for Kitty's affections. Harry later described Mick as 'a formidable opponent' in the battle for Kitty's hand. Their love triangle would continue on and off over the coming years.

The same year Michael had already begun to develop a web of spies throughout the British establishment, getting our own back for all the times the gougers had infiltrated Irish rebel forces. These tipped him off that the first meeting of Dáil Éireann was to be raided, but his warning was ignored and Dev and others were arrested. The remaining men met in January 1919 to convene the Dáil in the Mansion House and make the IRA the official army of the Irish Republic. On the same day, an IRA ambush in Tipperary resulted in two RIC men being shot dead. The War of Independence had begun.

In April, Michael masterminded Dev's escape from Lincoln Jail, and later that year Dev appointed him Minister for Finance. He proved an inspired choice and organised a bond issue called the National Loan that raised £400,000, which could buy a lot of pints in those days. That year also, Dev decided to take himself (and Harry) off to the USA to raise funds and try and get official recognition for the new state. Big Mick was miffed at Dev leaving in the middle of a war, but sort of delighted to have Harry out of the way, which would help in the other war – for Kitty's heart.

Michael's leadership and strategic skills saw him appointed Director of Intelligence of the IRA, effectively putting him in charge of running the war. He expanded his network of spies, who often came in the shape of secretaries, clerks and chambermaids, and he organised 'flying columns' all over the country, who would strike a target and then get the hell away before the British knew what had hit them. In late 1919 the British Government sent in the hated 'Black and Tans' to try and get control of the situation – but their brutality only escalated things.

In the summer of 1920, Michael set up 'The Squad' – trained and trusted men tasked with assassinating British agents. These men were also nicknamed the 'Apostles', and they religiously wiped out one British agent after another that year, becoming a serious thorn in the British establishment's arse. In November the Squad went after the group of agents known as 'The Cairo Gang', who were specially trained agents brought in to try and flush out Michael, who now had a £10,000 reward on his head. On November 21st 1920, the Squad assassinated 14 of these agents. The British responded by sending troops into Croke Park during a Dublin versus Tipperary match. They opened fire on the crowd, massacring 14 unarmed civilians. They also murdered three IRA prisoners in Dublin Castle. It was the first of Ireland's 'Bloody Sundays'.

Yet they couldn't capture The Big Fellow, who cycled about the country in disguise, often as a priest, living in safe houses and barns. The IRA's guerrilla tactics continued unabated and the British realised the war was unwinnable. British PM Lloyd George decided on a different tactic – peace talks. A truce was called in July 1921.

Dev was back from the States by now, but controversially decided to send Michael and Arthur Griffith (P308) as the chief negotiators, despite the fact that he was the most experienced politician in Ireland. Michael didn't want to go: 'I'm a soldier, not a politician.' But he relented, all too aware that he was probably being set up as a scapegoat should things not work out.

He was back and forth to London in the coming months, and during one trip home he met up with Kitty in the Grand Hotel in Greystones, Wicklow, where he popped the question. Kitty

Michael pops the question to Kitty

accepted. Harry was finally out of the picture. They decided to wed as soon as the war was over.

When the lads finally returned with the Treaty in December that year, Dev and friends were not happy, and Michael said of it that he had signed his own death warrant. Ireland would have 'dominion' status meaning we'd have our own parliament but still have to swear loyalty to the king. But worst of all in Dev's view was that six counties in the north were to remain completely under British rule. But to Big Mick, it gave us 'the freedom to achieve freedom'. When the

Treaty was debated in the Dáil and passed by just seven votes, those opposed to it walked out, led by Dev himself, full steam ahead for another war.

On January 16th 1922, Michael Collins, now commander-in-chief of the newly formed Free State Army, arrived at Dublin Castle to accept the handover of power. The Lord Lieutenant, Lord Fitzalan reputedly said: 'You are seven minutes late, Mr Collins', to which The Big Fellow replied: 'We've been waiting over 700 years, you can have the extra seven minutes'.

In April 1922, a large group of anti-Treaty insurgents took over the Four Courts in Dublin. After negotiations failed, the Free State Army, probably acting directly under Michael Collins' orders, began shelling the building. The Civil War had started. Over the coming days, the Four Courts and much of O'Connell Street was destroyed – and the feckin' street had only just been rebuilt after the Rising.

Over the following year the war divided the country, with tit for tat killings, executions, assassinations and general mayhem. But Michael would not live to see its end. By August of 1922 he was determined to restore peace and was prepared to allow anti-Treaty forces to 'go home without their arms, without surrendering their principles', as long as they would accept the Treaty.

But on August 22nd, when driving in convoy through the place called Béal na mBlath in Cork, an ambush ensued. He was struck in the head and died instantly. To this day no one knows for sure who ordered or carried out the killing. Conspiracy theories abound, the main one being that Dev was behind it, but there's no evidence for that.

Michael's body lay in state for three days as countless thousands filed past. Kitty was completely distraught and would spend the following year in mourning. Michael's funeral cortege was witnessed by half a million people, one fifth of the population. He was buried in Glasnevin Cemetery.

Kitty would marry a man called Felix Cronin in 1925. They had two sons, one of whom she called Michael Collins Cronin. She died of Bright's Disease in 1945 and was buried close to Michael in Glasnevin.

An annual commemoration takes place at the spot where Michael fell, and a monument marks the spot. He was the subject of two movies, one in 1936 called *Beloved Enemy* starring David Niven and, of course, the blockbuster *Michael Collins* starring Liam Neeson.

Oh, and also starring Julia Roberts as Kitty (sweet Jaysus almighty.)

Given his status in Irish history, you'd expect there'd be a gansey-load of statues all over the place. But no, the only proper one is in Clonakilty, Cork. There are a few busts, GAA clubs and a museum named in his honour. One suspects there wasn't much enthusiasm in Dev's party, Fianna Fáil, for spending money on statues of Collins. But really, seriously, if it were any other country in the world, there would be a ginormous statue in the centre of the country's capital. Perhaps in the centenary years ahead someone will finally get the finger out and properly commemorate Ireland's Lost Leader.

KEVIN O'HIGGINS

(1892–1927)

If you want to stir up a row just for the craic, just mention the name of Kevin O'Higgins to a group of historically knowledgeable Irish folk, then sit back and watch the sparks fly. Because Kevin was undoubtedly a love-hate figure, depending on your point of view. He was also one of the most prominent statesmen in the early years of the state.

Is that incense or Woodbines I smell, O'Higgins?

Born in Laois, Kevin was groomed early on for the priesthood, but was chucked out of Maynooth College for breaking the non-smoking rules! So he went to UCD to become a solicitor, who were allowed smoke themselves to death. In between lectures he joined the Irish Volunteers and made speeches that upset the Brits, who threw him in Mountjoy for five months, giving the law student a first-hand experience of injustice. On his release, now with a fire in his belly, he stood for election for Sinn Féin in Laois in 1918 and won.

Senior political positions soon followed and he became a passionate advocate of the Anglo-Irish Treaty. By 1922 he was Minister for Economic Affairs and he was responsible for many of Ireland's early infrastructural projects. His legal brain came in handy when the lads were drafting our constitution and he was one of its principal authors.

His ministerial portfolio soon included Justice, and this is where made himself unpopular with half of Ireland, as he played a prominent role in the execution of 77 republicans in the Civil War, one of whom, Rory O'Connor, had been the best man at Kevin's own wedding! He clearly wasn't a guy to mess about with, but then neither were fanatical republicans, who responded by murdering his father and torching his home.

Another decision made Kevin unpopular with almost the entire nation, when he reduced pub opening hours by a third. The horror! But perhaps his greatest legacy to the state was the founding of

That's great – now we only have time for 8 pints instead of our usual 12.

our unarmed civic guard, known now as An Garda Síochána, to put all the bad guys like thieves, murderers, extortionists, crooked bankers and bent politicians into prison. Ok, scratch the last two.

Unfortunately for Kevin, republican memories are not short and on Sunday, July 10th 1927, he was walking to mass in Booterstown, Co. Dublin, when he was shot dead by three IRA assassins. In 2012, Taoiseach Enda Kenny unveiled a plaque at the spot where he died.

LIAM LYNCH

(1893–1923)

It's a shame that so many heroes of the War of Independence ended their days as hunted outlaws in their own country. Well, war's a bitch, as they say, and it certainly was to Liam.

Born in Limerick, he apprenticed in the hardware trade, but soon exchanged the pots and pans for a different sort of hardware: rifles and grenades. By 1915, he was a full-time Volunteer, but didn't take any significant part in the Rising. He did, however, witness some violent shootings of nationalists by members of the RIC, and decided to dedicate his life thereafter to payback.

During the War of Independence he was in command of the IRA's very active Cork No. 2 Brigade, and he became the British Army's number one target in the south. Thanks to the his success and strategic skills, he was appointed to the IRB's Supreme Council in early 1921, and also made Divisional Commandant of the IRA's Southern Division. He continued to do battle and outwit the British, but ammunition was running low and increasing numbers of enemy soldiers were swarming the southern counties, so it was with a huge sigh of relief that he greeted the truce in July of that year.

The Treaty, however, he met with a huge sigh of exasperation. He was bitterly opposed to the abandonment of a republic, but tried desperately to find a compromise and prevent the impending Civil War. When the shells started raining down on the Four Courts in April 1922, he knew his efforts had failed.

He escaped and fled south, and was made Chief of Staff of the anti-Treaty forces, personally taking command of the Southern Division. He even had a plan (which seems a bit barmy from a present day perspective) that involved setting up a new 'Republic of Munster', operating as an independent country on

the island of Ireland. But the Munster Republic was not to be, as the Free State Troops began to take command of the towns one by one, forcing Liam and co further and further south.

Increasingly under pressure, Liam sanctioned the assassination of Free State TDs and various other prominent members of the new state in response to the execution of anti-Treaty republicans. The development brought a new level of bitterness to the war, as one atrocity, either official or unofficial, led to another in reprisal. Yep, it turned out we could be just as brutal as the British when we felt like it.

By March 1923, some senior anti-Treaty leaders, Dev included, wanted to end the war. Liam didn't, and he persuaded them to carry on. In his case, it would be to the bitter end.

A month later and things had gone from bad to wojus for his forces. While travelling to Cork, Liam and his men were intercepted by Free State troops near the Knockmealdown Mountains, and fled into the hills. A column of soldiers caught up with them and opened fire, seriously wounding Liam. He was carrying important documents so ordered his men to take them and leave him behind. The Free State soldiers took him to a hospital in Clonmel, but he died that night.

He was buried in Fermoy, Cork. His death effectively brought an end to the Civil War, and a couple of weeks later the anti-Treaty forces declared a ceasefire.

In 1935, probably the single biggest monument to anyone involved in the Rising or War of Independence was erected in Liam Lynch's honour, although 99.99% of the Irish people have never seen it. That's because it's where Liam fell, halfway up a mountain in the middle of a forest. It's

The Liam Lynch Memorial

a pretty impressive 60ft round tower surrounded by four bronze wolfhounds. The uniform he wore that day, complete with bullet hole, is on display in Dublin's Collins Barracks – named after the man who was Liam Lynch's enemy.

TOM BARRY

(1897–1980)

Many of those who fought in the War of Independence were labourers, farmers and shopkeepers and hadn't a clue about military strategy. Tom Barry, probably the most famous of the IRA's guerrilla commanders, was the exception, for he was not only trained, but trained by the British!

Born in Killorglin, Co. Kerry, his father had been in the RIC, the sworn enemies of the nationalists, but Barry Senior left the police force to open a shop in Cork when Tom was just a chiseller. When WW1 arrived, Tom enlisted in the British Army – he said himself he had no real interest either in Irish history, or in the British Empire, but joined up because he

Don't be silly Tommy. Of course you can't be a gorilla when you grow up.

wanted to see the world, use a gun and become a man.

And he certainly got around, though he may not have taken in the sights, being preoccupied with not getting his head blown off. His tours took him to Mesopotamia (Iraq), Egypt, Jerusalem, Italy and France. While in Mesopotamia he read the news about the Easter Rising and it dawned on him that he was in the very army who'd brutally suppressed his countrymen.

Back in Ireland in 1919, he realised he'd finished one war only to join another, but this time opposing his old comrades. In 1920 he joined the IRA, who recognised that his experience would come in very handy. He became involved in training butchers, bakers and barmen to become soldiers, and his West Cork brigade became renowned for its discipline and skill.

After loads of successful but minor guerrilla raids, he decided that it was time for a big one. He wanted to attack a platoon of Auxiliaries, a hated paramilitary unit of the RIC, who had been responsible for brutal reprisal attacks against civilians. He positioned 36 of his men either side of a road near Kilmichael, Cork, and then personally stood on the road in an IRA uniform waiting for the Auxiliary convoy to approach. When the first truck slowed he threw a grenade into it and wiped out half the men inside. A long gunfight ensued, and the Auxiliaries were virtually wiped out. The Irish lost three men, the enemy 17.

And over the coming year, he led so many successful guerrilla raids that he became a major pain in the arse for the British, who simply couldn't exercise control despite having almost 15,000 troops in the county.

Tom was bitterly opposed to the 1921 Anglo-Irish Treaty. He fought against the Free State forces in Dublin in the Civil War, which earned him a trip to prison in Meath. He duly managed to escape, return south and put his strategic genius to use against former comrades yet again, successfully mounting countless raids across Munster. But as the war progressed, he began to realise it was futile and wanted a ceasefire to prevent further deaths. He was captured again just before the war's end, and spent another year in prison.

Tom Barry's wars were not over, however. While he worked at a nice day job as superintendent of Cork Harbour Commission for the next 40 years, he continued to be involved in IRA activities, including the assassination in 1936 of Henry Summerville, a retired British Vice-Admiral who had been trying to recruit local men into the Royal Navy. And during WW2 he was one of several IRA men who had dealings with the Germans – arms in return for attacking British military targets.

Tom published his memoirs in 1949, his book providing historians with lots of gritty detail from the War of Independence. The famous Kilmichael ambush inspired a scene in Ken Loach's movie *The Wind that Shakes the Barley* and there are large memorials recalling both Kilmichael and Crossbarry, in memory of the men who fought for Ireland's freedom, led by General Tom Barry.

ERNIE O'MALLEY

(1897–1957)

Not only is he the inspiration for a great movie in the noughties, but he was also the consultant on another classic Irish movie in the fifties, and a literary wiz himself. Not bad for a rebel who almost shook hands with the Grim Reaper more than once.

Born in Castlebar, Mayo, to well-off Catholic parents, Ernie's father was a civil servant and the family had lots of connections to the British establishment – his first cousin would later become the British ambassador to Ireland. Not a good start for a rebel.

When he was 10 the family moved to Dublin. He proved to be a bright spark, later earning a place in UCD where he studied medicine. During the Rising, he refused to join in the defence of Trinity College against the rebels, choosing instead to covertly fire at the British. Within a year he'd joined the IRA and the only operations he'd be performing after that were of the guerrilla type.

A natural leader, when the War of Independence kicked off, he led successful missions all over the country, including the capture of an RIC barracks in Monaghan and a British Army barracks in Mallow, which yielded a gansey-load of weapons. The British responded by burning half of Mallow to the ground i.e. taking it out on the civilians.

Ernie was a tough cookie. After two years of really pissing off the British, he was eventually nabbed in Kilkenny, beaten to a pulp in Dublin Castle, and then thrown in Kilmainham to await execution. But he escaped and resumed his duties as if nothing had happened. He devotion and courage meant he was adored by his men.

Not surprisingly, he was against the Anglo-Irish Treaty and was among those besieged in the Four Courts in Dublin in 1922, which heralded the start of the Civil War. He escaped that time, but six months later, received 20 bullet wounds in a shoot-out in

Ballsbridge. He spent 18 months in a hospital prison, during which time he got himself elected as a TD for Dublin North.

In 1928 Dev (P351) dispatched him on a fundraising mission to the USA. Clearly broadening his horizons big time, he spent several years stateside, and lived with a tribe of native Indians in New Mexico, before getting in with a literary and arty circle that included DH Lawrence.

This no doubt inspired Ernie to lift a pen of his own, and he began work on his autobiographical book *On Another Man's Wound*. He also formed a long-standing relationship with a sculptor called Helen Hooker. He found a publisher in London for his

book, although the gougers left out the bits about him being tortured by the British. The great Irish contemporary writer John McGahern would later describe the book as 'the one classic work to have emerged directly from the violence that led to independence'. High praise indeed.

Ernie moved back to Mayo in 1938 and became a farmer. In between dipping sheep, he worked on the second volume of his memoirs, concerning the Civil War, called *The Singing Flame*, which wouldn't be published until after his death. He left tons of detailed notes, which proved to be like gold dust for later researchers. His literary and intellectual pursuits brought him to the attention of movie director John Ford, who asked him to act as consultant on the classic 'Oirish' movie *The Quiet Man*.

But, despite his full life, Ernie had never fully recovered from his multiple gunshot wounds and was aged just 60 when he died. He was given a state funeral and is buried at Glasnevin. Another hugely successful movie, *The Wind That Shakes the Barley* (2006), starring Cillian Murphy, was largely inspired by his experiences. Indeed Ernie was a genuine star in his own right.

KEVIN BARRY

(1902–1920)

~

But a lad of 18 summers,
Still there's no-one can deny,
As he walked to death that morning,
He proudly held his head on high.

In 1920, the British handed those fighting the War of Independence their single biggest recruiting tool, when they executed the 18-year-old Kevin Barry.

Born in Fleet Street, Dublin, Kevin spent half his time there and the other half in Carlow, where his mother hailed from. By the age of 13, he was already rarin' to go to battle, as evidenced by his attendance at a Manchester Martyrs event, commemorating nationalists who'd been executed in England in 1867. He witnessed first-hand his home's destruction during the Easter Rising. The following year, he signed up with the Volunteers, aged just 15, and moved up the ranks when it became the IRA in 1919.

He was a keen hurler and rugby player, and had brains to burn, which resulted in him winning a

The Kevin Barry interview

scholarship to UCD to study medicine. But even as he was learning one thing by day, he was learning something quite different by night, taking part in raids on British targets during the War of Independence. He was promoted to Section Commander at just 18.

On September 20th 1920, he took part in the ambush of a British truck in Bolton Street, the intention being to seize weapons, but the operation went arseways and a gun battle ensued, resulting in the deaths of three British soldiers.

Kevin was captured, taken to Mountjoy and there endured physical beatings in an attempt to make him give up his comrades, but he never uttered a word. There was public outrage to reports of the torture, and there was outright disbelief when he was sentenced to death. International appeals wouldn't move the British, including those of USA diplomats and the Vatican. Michael Collins actually planned a rescue attempt, but the British brought in hundreds of reinforcements, so the plan was scrapped, which the Big Fellow bitterly regretted for the rest of his days.

Kevin's request to be executed by firing squad as a soldier, and not hanged, was refused, and when the Brits couldn't locate a hangman in Ireland willing to do the dirty work, they brought in John Ellis from Rochdale, England. Shortly before his execution, Kevin said: 'It is nothing, to give one's life for Ireland. What's my life compared with the cause?' He was calm and dignified as he went to his death, on November 1st, 1920.

His death sent countless young men flocking to the IRA. Once again the British had completely misjudged the Irish mood and mentality. Young Kevin's courage and sacrifice became the stuff of republican legend.

There is a monument to Kevin Barry in the Carlow village of Rathvilly. There's also a commemorative stained glass window in Earlsfort Terrace (formerly UCD), and a whole bunch of GAA clubs, including one in Connecticut, USA, named after him.

But what probably immortalised Kevin the most was the song written in his honour soon after his death. It has been performed by a gansey-load of folk bands and also by Leonard Cohen. Here's the final verse:

Another martyr for old Ireland,
Another murder for the Crown,
Whose brutal laws to crush the Irish,
Could not keep their spirit down.
Lads like Barry are no cowards.
From the foe they will not fly.
Lads like Barry will free Ireland,
For her sake they'll live and die.